Assessment Guide

Module K

HOLT McDOUGAL

HOUGHTON MIFFLIN HARCOURT

Acknowledgements for Covers

Cover Photo Credits

Micro-circuit board (bg) ©Roger Du Buisson/Corbis; *tweezer* (l) ©Corbis; *bulbs* (cl) ©Peter Gridley/Photographer's Choice RF/Getty Images; *wind tunnel* (cr) ©George Steinmetz/Corbis; *bioscience* (r) ©Andrew Brookes/Corbis

Printed in the U.S.A.

ISBN   978-0-547-59350-0

 2 3 4 5 6 7 8 9 10   0982   20 19 18 17 16 15 14 13 12 11
4500309789   A B C D E F G

Contents

Unit 2 Measurement and Data

Unit 3 Engineering, Technology, and Society

End-of-Module Test

Answer Sheet

Answer Key

INTRODUCTION
Overview

ScienceFusion provides parallel instructional paths for teaching important science content. You may choose to use the print path, the digital path, or a combination of the two. The quizzes, tests, and other resources in this Assessment Guide may be used with either path.

The *ScienceFusion* assessment options are intended to give you maximum flexibility in assessing what your students know and what they can do. The program's formative and summative assessment categories reflect the understanding that assessment is a learning opportunity for students, and that students must periodically demonstrate mastery of content in cumulative tests.

All *ScienceFusion* tests are available—and editable—in ExamView and online at thinkcentral.com. You can customize a quiz or test for your classroom in many ways:

- adding or deleting items
- adjusting for cognitive complexity, Bloom's taxonomy level, or other measures of difficulty
- changing the sequence of items
- changing the item formats
- editing the question itself

All of these changes, except the last, can be made without invalidating the content correlation of the item.

This Assessment Guide is your directory to assessment in *ScienceFusion*. In it you'll find copymasters for Lesson Quizzes, Unit Tests, Unit Reviews, Performance-Based Assessments Alternative Assessments, and End-of-Module Tests; answers and explanations of answers; rubrics; a bubble-style answer sheet; and suggestions for assessing student progress using performance, portfolio, and other forms of integrated assessment.

You will also find additional assessment prompts and ideas throughout the program, as indicated on the chart that follows.

Assessment in *ScienceFusion* Program

	Student Editions	Teacher Edition	Assessment Guide	Digital Lessons	Online Resources at thinkcental.com	ExamView Test Generator
Formative Assessment						
Assessing Prior Knowledge						
Engage Your Brain	X					
Unit Pretest			X		X	X
Embedded Assessment						
Active Reading Questions	X					
Interactivities	X					
Probing Questions		X				
Formative Assessment		X				
Classroom Discussions		X				
Common Misconceptions		X				
Learning Alerts		X				
Embedded Questions and Tasks				X		
Student Self-Assessments				X		
Digital Lesson Quiz				X		
When used primarily for teaching						
Lesson Review	X	X				
Lesson Quiz			X		X	X
Alternative Assessment			X		X	
Performance-Based Assessment			X			
Portfolio Assessment, guidelines			X			
Summative Assessment						
End of Lessons						
Visual Summary	X	X				
Lesson Quiz			X		X	X
Alternative Assessment		X	X		X	
Rubrics			X		X	
End of Units						
Unit Review	X		X		X	X
Answers		X	X		X	
Test Doctor Answer Explanations		X	X			X
Unit Test A (on level)			X		X	X
Unit Test B (below level)			X		X	X
End of Module						
End-of-Module Test			X		X	X

Formative Assessment
Assessing Prior Knowledge

Frequently in this program, you'll find suggestions for assessing what your students already know before they begin studying a new lesson. These activities help you warm up the class, focus minds, and activate students' prior knowledge.

In This Assessment Guide

Each of the units begins with a Unit Pretest consisting of multiple-choice questions that assess prior and prerequisite knowledge. Use the Pretest to get a snapshot of the class and help you organize your pre-teaching.

In the Student Edition

Engage Your Brain Simple, interactive warm-up tasks get students thinking, and remind them of what they may already know about the lesson topics.

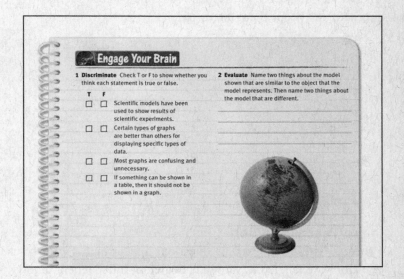

Active Reading Questions Students first see the lesson vocabulary on the opening page, where they are challenged to show what they know about the terms. Multiple exposures to the key terms throughout the lesson lead to mastery.

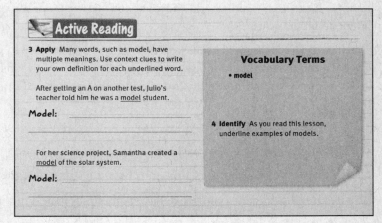

In the Teacher Edition

Opening Your Lesson At the start of each TE lesson Opening Your Lesson suggests questions and activities that help you assess prerequisite and prior knowledge.

Embedded Assessment

Once you're into the lesson, you'll continue to find suggestions, prompts, and resources for ongoing assessment.

Student Edition

Active Reading Questions and Interactivities Frequent questions and interactive prompts are embedded in the text, where they give students instant feedback on their comprehension. They ask students to respond in different ways, such as writing, drawing, and annotating the text. The variety of skills and response types helps all students succeed, and keeps them interested.

Active Reading 5 **Define** Write an original definition for the term *data*.

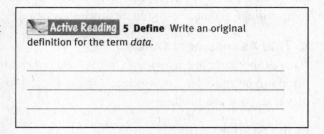

Movie Tickets Sold Monthly

Month	Number of Tickets
January	15,487
February	12,654
March	15,721
April	10,597
May	10,916
June	11,797
July	18,687
August	18,302
September	16,978
October	10,460
November	11,807
December	17,497

6 **Extend** What other kind of data could you collect at home that might show differences over the course of a year?

In the Teacher Edition

Probing Questions Probing questions appear in the point-of-use teaching suggestions. These questions are labeled to show the degree of independent inquiry they require. The three levels of inquiry—Directed, Guided, and Independent—give students experience that builds toward independent analysis.

Classroom Discussions Discussion is a natural opportunity to gauge how well students have absorbed the material, and to assess any misconceptions or gaps in their understanding. Students also learn from each other in this informal exchange. Classroom discussion ideas appear throughout the lesson in the Teacher Edition.

Tips for Classroom Discussions

- Allow students plenty of time to reflect and formulate their answers.

- Call upon students you sense have something to add but who haven't spoken.

- At the same time, allow reluctant students not to speak unless they choose to.

- Encourage students to respond to each other as well as to you.

Misconceptions and Learning Alerts The Teacher Background pages at the start of a unit describe common misconceptions and identify the lessons in which the misconceptions can be addressed. Strategies for addressing the misconceptions appear in the point-of-use teaching notes. Additional Learning Alerts help you introduce and assess challenging topics.

Formative Assessment A final formative assessment strategy appears on the Evaluate page at the end of each lesson, followed by reteaching ideas.

In This Assessment Guide

Several of the assessment strategies described in this book can be used either as formative or as summative instruments, depending on whether you use them primarily for teaching or primarily for evaluation. The choice is yours. Among these are the Lesson Quizzes, described here, and the Alternative Assessment, described under Summative Assessment, next. Because both of these assessments are provided for every lesson, you could use them both at different times.

Lesson Quizzes as Formative Assessment In this book, Lesson Quizzes in a unit follow the Unit Pretest. The five-item Lesson Quiz can be administered as a written test, used as an oral quiz, or given to small student groups for collaboration. In the Answer Key at the end of this book, you'll find a feature called the Test Doctor, which provides a brief explanation of what makes each correct answer correct and each incorrect answer incorrect. Use this explanatory material to begin a discussion following the quiz.

Classroom Observation

Classroom observation is one way to gather and record information that can lead to improved instruction. You'll find a Classroom Observation Checklist in Assessment Tools, following the Introduction.

Tips for Classroom Observation

- Don't try to see and record everything at once. Instead, identify specific skills you will observe in a session.

- Don't try to observe everyone at once. Focus on a few students at a time.

- Repeat observations at different times in order to identify patterns. This practice helps you validate or correct your impressions from a single time.

- Use the checklist as is or modify it to suit your students and your instruction. Fill in student names across the top and write the date next to the skills you are observing on a particular day.

- Keep the checklist, add to it, and consult it periodically for hints about strengths, weaknesses, and developments of particular students and of the class.

- Use your own system of ratings or the simple number code on the checklist. When you have not seen enough to give a rating, leave the space blank.

Summative Assessment

In the Student Edition

Visual Summary and Lesson Review

Interactive summaries help students synthesize lesson material, and the Lesson Review provides a variety of questions focusing on vocabulary, key concepts, and critical thinking.

Unit Reviews

Each unit in the Student Edition is followed by a Unit Review, also available in this Assessment Guide. These tests include the item types commonly found on the statewide assessments. You may want to use these tests to review unit content right away or at any time later in the year to help students prepare for the statewide assessment. If you wish to give students practice in filling in a machine-scorable answer sheet, use the bubble-type answer sheet at the start of the Answer Key.

In This Assessment Guide

Alternative Assessments

Every lesson has an Alternative Assessment worksheet, which is previewed in the Teacher Edition on the Evaluate page of the lesson. The activities on these worksheets assess student comprehension of core content, while at the same time offering a variety of options for students with various abilities, learning styles, and interests. The activities require students to produce a tangible product or to give a presentation that demonstrates their understanding of skills and concepts.

Tips for Alternative Assessment

- The structure of these worksheets allows for differentiation in topic, difficulty level, and activity type/learner preferences.

- Each worksheet has a variety of items for students and teachers to choose from.

- The items may relate to the entire lesson content or to just one or two key topics. Encourage students to select items so that they will hit most key topics in a lesson.

- Share the rubrics and Presentation Guidelines with students so they understand the expectations for these assignments. You could have them fill in a rubric with their name and activity choices at the same time they choose their assignments, and then submit the rubric with their presentation or assignment.

Grading Alternative Assessments

Each type of Alternative Assessment worksheet has a rubric for easy grading.

- The rubrics focus mostly on content comprehension, but also take into account presentation.

- The Answer Key describes the expected content mastery for each Alternative Assessment.

- Separate Presentation Guidelines describe the attributes of successful written work, posters and displays, oral presentations, and multimedia presentations.

- Each rubric has space to record your reasons for deducting points, such as content errors or particular presentation flaws.

- If you wish to change the focus of an Alternative Assessment worksheet, you can adjust the point values for the rubric.

The Presentation Guidelines and the rubrics follow the Introduction. The Answer Key appears at the end of the book.

Unit Tests A and B

This Assessment Guide contains leveled tests for each unit.

- The A-level tests are for students who typically perform below grade level.

- The B-level tests are intended for students whose performance is on grade level.

Both versions of the test address the unit content with a mixture of item types, including multiple choice, short response, and extended response. Both levels contains items of low, medium, and high cognitive complexity, though level B contains more items of higher complexity. A few items appear in both of the tests as a means of assuring parallel content coverage. If you need a higher-level test, you can easily assemble one from the lesson assessment banks in ExamView or online at thinkcentral.com. All items in the banks are tagged with five different measures of difficulty as well as standards and key terms.

End-of-Module Test

The final test in this Assessment Guide is the End-of-Module Review. This is a long-form, multiple-choice test in the style of the statewide assessments. An Answer Sheet appears with the review.

Performance-Based Assessment

Performance-Based Assessment involves a hands-on activity in which students demonstrate their skills and thought processes. Each Performance-Based Assessment includes a page of teacher-focused information and a general rubric for scoring. In addition to the Performance-Based Assessment provided for each unit, you can use many of the labs in the program as the basis for performance assessment.

Tips for Performance Assessment

- Prepare materials and stations so that all students have the same tasks. You may want to administer performance assessments to different groups over time.

- Provide clear expectations, including the measures on which students will be evaluated. You may invite them to help you formulate or modify the rubric.

- Assist students as needed, but avoid supplying answers to those who can handle the work on their own.

- Don't be hurried. Allow students enough time to do their best work.

Developing or Modifying a Rubric

Developing a rubric for a performance task involves three basic steps:

1. Identify the inquiry skills that are taught in the lesson and that students must perform to complete the task successfully and identify the understanding of content that is also required. Many of the skills may be found in the Lab and Activity Evaluation later in this guide.

2. Determine which skills and understandings of content are involved in each step.

3. Decide what you will look for to confirm that the student has acquired each skill and understanding you identified.

Portfolio Assessment, Guidelines

A portfolio is a showcase for student work, a place where many types of assignments, projects, reports and data sheets can be collected. The work samples in the collection provide snapshots of the student's efforts over time, and taken together they reveal the student's growth, attitudes, and understanding better than other types of assessment. Portfolio assessment involves meeting with each student to discuss the work and to set goals for future performance. In contrast with formal assessments, portfolio assessments have these advantages:

1. They give students a voice in the assessment process.

2. They foster reflection, self-monitoring, and self-evaluation.

3. They provide a comprehensive picture of a student's progress.

Tips for Portfolio Assessment

- Make a basic plan. Decide how many work samples will be included in the portfolios and what period of time they represent.

- Explain the portfolio and its use. Describe the portfolio an artist might put together, showing his or her best or most representative work, as part of an application for school or a job. The student's portfolio is based on this model.

- Together with your class decide on the required work samples that everyone's portfolio will contain.

- Explain that the students will choose additional samples of their work to include. Have students remember how their skills and understanding have grown over the period covered by the portfolio, and review their work with this in mind. The best pieces to choose may not be the longest or neatest.

- Give students the Portfolio Planning Worksheet found in Assessment Tools. Have students record their reasoning as they make their selections and assemble their portfolios.

- Share with students the Portfolio Evaluation Checklist, also found in Assessment Tools, and explain how you will evaluate the contents of their portfolios.

- Use the portfolios for conferences, grading, and planning. Give students the option of taking their portfolios home to share.

ASSESSMENT TOOLS
Alternative Assessment Presentation Guidelines

The following guidelines can be used as a starting point for evaluating student presentation of alternative assessments. For each category, use only the criteria that are relevant for the particular format you are evaluating; some criteria will not apply for certain formats.

Written Work
- Matches the assignment in format (essay, journal entry, newspaper report, etc.)
- Begins with a clear statement of the topic and purpose
- Provides information that is essential to the reader's understanding
- Supporting details are precise, related to the topic, and effective
- Follows a logical pattern of organization
- Uses transitions between ideas
- When appropriate, uses diagrams or other visuals
- Correct spelling, capitalization, and punctuation
- Correct grammar and usage
- Varied sentence structures
- Neat and legible

Posters and Displays
- Matches the assignment in format (brochure, poster, storyboard, etc.)
- Topic is well researched and quality information is presented
- Poster communicates an obvious, overall message
- Posters have large titles and the message, or purpose, is obvious
- Images are big, clear, and convey important information
- More important ideas and items are given more space and presented with larger images or text
- Colors are used for a purpose, such as to link words and images
- Sequence of presentation is easy to follow because of visual cues, such as arrows, letters, or numbers
- Artistic elements are appropriate and add to the overall presentation
- Text is neat
- Captions and labels have correct spelling, capitalization, and punctuation

Oral Presentations
- Matches the assignment in format (speech, news report, etc.)
- Presentation is delivered well, and enthusiasm is shown for topic
- Words are clearly pronounced and can easily be heard
- Information is presented in a logical, interesting sequence that the audience can follow
- Visual aids are relative to content, very neat, and artistic
- Often makes eye contact with audience
- Listens carefully to questions from the audience and responds accurately
- Stands straight, facing the audience
- Uses movements appropriate to the presentation; does not fidget
- Covers the topic well in the time allowed
- Gives enough information to clarify the topic, but does not include irrelevant details

Multimedia Presentations
- Topic is well researched, and essential information is presented
- The product shows evidence of an original and inventive approach
- The presentation conveys an obvious, overall message
- Contains all the required media elements, such as text, graphics, sounds, videos, and animations
- Fonts and formatting are used appropriately to emphasize words; color is used appropriately to enhance the fonts
- Sequence of presentation is logical and/or the navigation is easy and understandable
- Artistic elements are appropriate and add to the overall presentation
- The combination of multimedia elements with words and ideas produces an effective presentation
- Written elements have correct spelling, capitalization, and punctuation

Alternative Assessment Rubric – Tic-Tac-Toe

Worksheet Title: _____

Student Name: _____

Date: _____

Add the titles of each activity chosen to the chart below.

	Content (0-3 points)	**Presentation** (0-2 points)	*Points Sum*
Choice 1: _____			
Points			
Reason for missing points			
Choice 2: _____			
Points			
Reason for missing points			
Choice 3: _____			
Points			
Reason for missing points			
		Total Points (of 15 maximum)	

Alternative Assessment Rubric – Mix and Match

Worksheet Title: _____

Student Name: _____

Date: _____

Add the column choices to the chart below.

	Content (0-3 points)	**Presentation** (0-2 points)	*Points Sum*
Information Source from Column A: _____ Topics Chosen for Column B: _____ _____ Presentation Format from Column C: _____			
Points			
Reason for missing points			
		Total Points (of 5 maximum)	

Alternative Assessment Rubric – Take Your Pick

Worksheet Title: _____

Student Name: _____

Date: _____

Add the titles of each activity chosen to the chart below.

	Content	**Presentation**	***Points Sum***
2-point item: 5-point item 8-point item:	*(0-1.5 points)* *(0-4 points)* *(0-6 points)*	*(0-0.5 point)* *(0-1 point)* *(0-2 points)*	
Choice 1: _____			
Points			
Reason for missing points			
Choice 2: _____			
Points			
Reason for missing points			
		Total Points (of 10 maximum)	

Alternative Assessment Rubric – Choose Your Meal

Worksheet Title: _____

Student Name: _____

Date: _____

Add the titles of each activity chosen to the chart below.

	Content	**Presentation**	*Points Sum*
Appetizer, side dish, or dessert:	*(0-3 points)*	*(0-2) points*	
Main Dish	*(0-6 points)*	*(0-4 points)*	
Appetizer: _____			
Points			
Reason for missing points			
Side Dish: _____			
Points			
Reason for missing points			
Main Dish: _____			
Points			
Reason for missing points			
Dessert: _____			
Points			
Reason for missing points			
		Total Points (of 25 maximum)	

Alternative Assessment Rubric – Points of View

Worksheet Title: _____

Student Name: _____

Date: _____

Add the titles of group's assignment to the chart below.

	Content (0-4 points)	Presentation (0-1 points)	Points Sum
Point of View:			
Points			
Reason for missing points			
		Total Points (of 5 maximum)	

Alternative Assessment Rubric – Climb the Pyramid

Worksheet Title: _____

Student Name: _____

Date: _____

Add the titles of each activity chosen to the chart below.

	Content *(0-3 points)*	**Presentation** *(0-2 points)*	***Points Sum***
Choice from bottom row: _____			
Points			
Reason for missing points			
Choice from middle row: _____			
Points			
Reason for missing points			
Top row: _____			
Points			
Reason for missing points			
		Total Points (of 15 maximum)	

Alternative Assessment Rubric – Climb the Ladder

Worksheet Title: _____

Student Name: _____

Date: _____

Add the titles of each activity chosen to the chart below.

	Content (0-3 points)	**Presentation** (0-2 points)	*Points Sum*
Choice 1 (top rung): _____			
Points			
Reason for missing points			
Choice 2 (middle rung): _____			
Points			
Reason for missing points			
Choice 3 (bottom rung): _____			
Points			
Reason for missing points			
		Total Points (of 15 maximum)	

Date _____

Rating Scale			
3	Outstanding	**1**	Needs Improvement
2	Satisfactory		Not Enough Opportunity to Observe

Names of Students **Inquiry Skills**											
Observe											
Compare											
Classify/Order											
Gather, Record, Display, or Interpret Data											
Use Numbers											
Communicate											
Plan and Conduct Simple Investigations											
Measure											
Predict											
Infer											
Draw Conclusions											
Use Time/Space Relationships											
Hypothesize											
Formulate or Use Models											
Identify and Control Variables											
Experiment											

Lab and Activity Evaluation

Circle the appropriate number for each criterion. Then add up the circled numbers in each column and record the sum in the subtotals row at the bottom. Add up these subtotals to get the total score.

Graded by _____ Total _____ /100

Behavior	Completely	Mostly	Partially	Poorly
Follows lab procedures carefully and fully	10–9	8–7–6	5–4–3	2–1–0
Wears the required safety equipment and displays knowledge of safety procedures and hazards	10–9	8–7–6	5–4–3	2–1–0
Uses laboratory time productively and stays on task	10–9	8–7–6	5–4–3	2–1–0
Behavior	**Completely**	**Mostly**	**Partially**	**Poorly**
Uses tools, equipment, and materials properly	10–9	8–7–6	5–4–3	2–1–0
Makes quantitative observations carefully, with precision and accuracy	10–9	8–7–6	5–4–3	2–1–0
Uses the appropriate SI units to collect quantitative data	10–9	8–7–6	5–4–3	2–1–0
Records accurate qualitative data during the investigation	10–9	8–7–6	5–4–3	2–1–0
Records measurements and observations in clearly organized tables that have appropriate headings and units	10–9	8–7–6	5–4–3	2–1–0
Works well with partners	10–9	8–7–6	5–4–3	2–1–0
Efficiently and properly solves any minor problems that might occur with materials or procedures	10–9	8–7–6	5–4–3	2–1–0
Subtotals:				

Comments

_____

_____

_____

_____

My Science Portfolio

What Is in My Portfolio	Why I Chose It
1.	
2.	
3.	
4.	
5.	
6.	
7.	

I organized my Science Portfolio this way because _____

_____

_____

_____

_____

Portfolio Evaluation Checklist

Aspects of Science Literacy	Evidence of Growth
1. **Understands science concepts** *(Animals, Plants; Earth's Land, Air, Water; Space; Weather; Matter, Motion, Energy)*	_____ _____ _____
2. **Uses inquiry skills** *(observes, compares, classifies, gathers/ interprets data, communicates, measures, experiments, infers, predicts, draws conclusions)*	_____ _____ _____
3. **Thinks critically** *(analyzes, synthesizes, evaluates, applies ideas effectively, solves problems)*	_____ _____ _____
4. **Displays traits/attitudes of a scientist** *(is curious, questioning, persistent, precise, creative, enthusiastic; uses science materials carefully; is concerned for environment)*	_____ _____ _____

Summary of Portfolio Assessment

For This Review			Since Last Review		
Excellent	Good	Fair	Improving	About the Same	Not as Good

Name _____ Date _____

The Nature of Science

Choose the letter of the best answer.

1. Scientists often make graphs to present their data. For example, the following graph shows the temperature of each planet in our solar system.

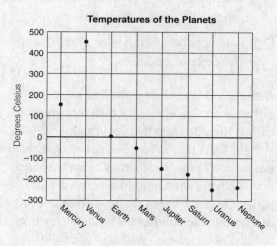

Temperatures of the Planets

Which kind of scientist would **most likely** make this graph?

A. an astronomer

B. an ecologist

C. an engineer

D. a geologist

2. Scientists conduct many types of scientific investigations. Their efforts often include fieldwork, surveys, models, and experiments. Which statement about scientific investigations is **true**?

A. They rarely involve the collection of data under controlled conditions.

B. They follow exactly the same steps because there is only one scientific method.

C. They include multiple trials to increase the consistency of the data that are collected.

D. Their primary focus seldom includes comparing or describing the unregulated world.

3. A biomedical company uses a certain type of bacteria to manufacture a new medicine. A researcher for the company studies how temperature affects the rate at which the bacteria reproduce. He records his results in a graph.

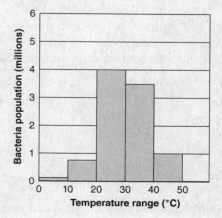

Currently, the company grows the bacteria in a lab maintained at 18 °C. If the company wants to grow the bacteria as quickly as possible, which recommendation should the researcher make?

A. The current lab temperature is ideal for growing the bacteria.

B. The lab temperature should be increased to between 20 °C and 30 °C.

C. The lab temperature should be increased to between 30 °C and 40 °C.

D. The lab temperature should be increased to between 40 °C and 50 °C.

4. Which phrase **best** defines science?

A. study of living organisms

B. observational study of Earth

C. discussion of feelings and thoughts

D. systematic study of natural events and conditions

5. Scientists depend upon various traits to carry out their work. An example is shown in the figure below.

Which of these terms **best** describes the scientist in this figure?

A. creative

B. logical

C. observant

D. skeptical

6. Florida A&M University has an Environmental Sciences Institute. In which area would research at this institute **most likely** have an impact?

A. weather prediction

B. new technology products

C. development of new medicines

D. conservation of natural resources

7. Diep did some research about classification for a science report. She learned that until 150 years ago, scientists recognized only two groups of organisms: plants and animals. Now, scientists also recognize several groups of microscopic organisms. How should Diep explain why scientists decided to classify organisms into more groups?

A. More types of organisms exist now than before.

B. Fewer organisms have gone extinct in recent years.

C. Scientists continue to learn more about living organisms.

D. Scientists invent new organisms that need to be classified.

8. Which of these answers best describes a scientific theory?

A. an explanation based on the opinion of a scientist

B. a well-supported and widely accepted explanation of nature

C. a description of a specific relationship under given conditions

D. a statement describing what always happens under certain conditions

9. A student is studying plants that grow in different areas and receive different levels of carbon dioxide from their environments. The student finds that in one area, plants have shown tremendous growth, whereas in another area, plants have shown little to no growth. The student hypothesizes that the different levels of carbon dioxide contributes to the differences noticed in the plants. Which of the following would best test this hypothesis?

A. a model that simulates weather and the water cycle in the plant areas

B. fieldwork to identify additional plant types in other areas

C. a controlled experiment in which the student attempts to control all variables except the carbon dioxide level

D. surveys of people on whether the plants they prefer to grow in their homes and gardens

10. Which title should be classified as pseudoscience?

A. *Is Life Possible on Mars?*

B. *Aliens Built the Pyramids!*

C. *The Best Ways for Making Money*

D. *The Disappearance of Ancient Civilizations in South America*

What Is Science?

Choose the letter of the best answer.

1. Which of the following is an example of a scientific claim?

   A. Numbers have symbolic meaning beyond their mathematical sense.

   B. According to data collected over the past hundred years, the global temperature of Earth is rising.

   C. One can determine the exact location of water underground by feeling the aura of the water with a forked stick.

   D. The future can be predicted by studying the position of the planets relative to the stars at a given moment.

2. The sixth-grader in this figure is displaying a trait that scientists must use in their work.

   Come to a conclusion

   Which trait does this figure **best** represent?

   A. curiosity

   B. objectivity

   C. skepticism

   D. logical reasoning

3. What limits what scientists can study in their work?

   A. They can study only the events that take place on Earth.

   B. They can study only phenomena that they can observe or model.

   C. They can investigate only questions that they were the first to ask.

   D. They can investigate only the areas of science in which they are experts.

4. Which of the following is a way pseudoscience differs from science?

   A. Pseudoscience does not follow the scientific method.

   B. Pseudoscience is limited to phenomena people can observe.

   C. Pseudoscience systematically studies natural events and conditions.

   D. Pseudoscience uses a large body of empirical evidence to make explanations.

5. What is the term for the cumulative body of observations on which scientific explanations are based?

   A. peer review

   B. pseudoscience

   C. logical reasoning

   D. empirical evidence

Scientific Investigations

Choose the letter of the best answer.

1. A researcher is trying to find information on the effects of computers on education. What source has the least validity?

   A. a paper in a professional education journal written by a scientist

   B. a story in a magazine written by a technology teacher with 20 years of experience

   C. a newspaper article by a journalist who cites the work of an educational researcher

   D. an article on the Internet by a scientist who did one study and used a small sample size

2. Scientific investigations involve many steps and processes. Which characteristics define a laboratory experiment?

   A. hypothesis, models, and calculations

   B. test variables, data, and uncontrolled conditions

   C. data, conclusions, and unregulated environment

   D. independent and dependent variables, data, and controlled conditions

3. Why might a scientist decide to do a laboratory experiment instead of fieldwork?

   A. to include a larger number of variables

   B. to make observations under natural conditions

   C. to make observations in a controlled environment

   D. to have a smaller sample size to observe and experiment on

4. Repetition is an important element of a good scientific investigation. Which data table has places to record information for repeated trials?

   A.

Distance traveled (m)	Time (s)	Average speed (m/s)

   B.

Time (min)	Temperature (°C)
0	
1	
2	
3	
4	
5	

   C.

Trial	Height (cm)	Distance traveled (cm)
1		
2		
3		
4		
5		

   D.

Initial temperature of water (°C)	
Final temperature of water (°C)	
Mass of water (g)	

5. New experimental data does not support a currently accepted hypothesis. Which course of action should the researcher take?

   A. Do the experiment until the results support the hypothesis.

   B. Change the data to fit the hypothesis.

   C. Form a new hypothesis and plan a new experiment.

   D. Change the procedure to obtain the desired outcome.

Scientific Knowledge

Choose the letter of the best answer.

1. Which statement describes how a scientist makes scientific explanations?

   A. A scientist bases scientific explanations on a large body of observations of the world.

   B. A scientist bases scientific explanations only on other scientists' opinions.

   C. A scientist bases scientific explanations on personal experience and opinions.

   D. A scientist suggests scientific explanations and makes up evidence to make them true.

2. The figure below shows a concept related to the kinetic theory of matter, which describes the behavior of gases based on the motion of the particles.

   10°C   20°C   30°C

   How would the kinetic theory explain what is happening in the above example?

   A. The balloon gets bigger as the temperature of the gas inside it decreases, because the gas particles move faster and get farther apart.

   B. The balloon gets smaller as the temperature of the gas inside it decreases, because the gas particles begin to escape from the balloon.

   C. The balloon gets bigger as the temperature of the gas inside it increases, because the gas particles move faster and get farther apart.

   D. The balloon gets smaller as the temperature of the gas inside it increases, because the gas particles move more slowly and get closer together.

3. Which of these scientists would most likely engage in fieldwork to observe organisms?

   A. chemist

   B. biologist

   C. physicist

   D. mathematician

4. Which of these events might lead to the modification of a scientific idea?

   A. A scientist uses a computer to teach a scientific concept to students.

   B. Two scientists doing the same experiment in different parts of the world under the same conditions get the same results.

   C. One scientist finds evidence that she feels doesn't fit a theory. Other scientists agree that her results are valid.

   D. A scientist performs an experiment and finds out that one of the chemicals used in the experiment was contaminated.

5. Simon is presenting a project on scientific laws and theories. Which of the following statements should he include to explain the differences between the two?

   A. Scientific theories requires scientific evidence but scientific laws do not.

   B. Scientific theories are based on observations and scientific laws are based on opinions.

   C. Scientific theories explain why something happens, and scientific laws describe what happens.

   D. Scientific theories are rarely changed and scientific laws are modified frequently.

Science and Society

Choose the letter of the best answer.

1. Scientific thought and investigation have had a tremendous impact on society. Which of the following scientific discoveries would have the **greatest** impact on society?

   A. discovery of a gold deposit

   B. discovery of a new species of animal

   C. discovery of a new star in the universe

   D. discovery of a way to prevent a disease

2. Some professions require scientific knowledge from more than one field. An example is shown in the following illustration.

   Which two fields of science must a person study to pursue the career shown in this illustration?

   A. biology and chemistry

   B. astronomy and biology

   C. geology and meteorology

   D. meteorology and chemistry

3. In 2008, Dr. Lydia Villa-Komaroff was named as the National Hispanic Scientist of the Year. In addition to her many contributions to society, she was a member of a research team that first showed that bacterial cells can be made to produce insulin. This discovery helps people, with diabetes, who take insulin to control their blood-sugar levels. In what area did Dr. Villa-Komaroff's work have an impact?

   A. medical treatments

   B. new technologies

   C. disease prevention

   D. conservation efforts

4. In which of the following is a mechanic acting most like a scientist?

   A. A mechanic eats a turkey sandwich and soup for lunch.

   B. A mechanic decides which type of oil would be best for a car.

   C. A mechanic uses robotic arms to lift a car in order to work underneath it.

   D. A mechanic makes an educated guess about why a car is not working, and then tests the guess.

5. Alexander Fleming was a Scottish scientist who discovered the antibiotic penicillin in 1928. In what area did Fleming's discovery have an impact?

   A. astronomy

   B. engineering

   C. treatment of diseases

   D. conservation practices

What Is Science?

Points of View: *Science*
Your class will work together to show what you've learned about science from several different viewpoints.

1. Work in groups as assigned by your teacher. Each group will be assigned to one or two viewpoints.

2. Complete your assignment, and present your perspective to the class.

 Examples Develop a multimedia presentation in which you describe life science, earth science, and physical science. Then, give three specific examples of something a scientist would study in each.

 Illustrations Draw a cartoon or comic strip of a scientist testing an idea of your choosing in either life science, earth science, or physical science. Be sure to include captions describing what your scientist is doing to test his or her ideas.

 Analysis Suppose that you are a scientist reviewing an article that has been submitted to a respected science journal for publication. In the article, the author claims that a combination of a homeopathic drug and a conventional chemotherapeutic drug cures leukemia, a cancer of the blood. How will you decide whether to treat the investigation as science or pseudoscience? Write an interview that might take place between you and the author.

 Observations One of the characteristics of science is making detailed observations. Choose two items in your classroom (such as a piece of chalk or paper) and develop a list of 10 observations for each. You may use various tools in your classroom such as a microscope or ruler. Then, describe how you made the observations and recorded the results. You should include at least one description in words, numbers and units, and sketch or diagram for each item.

 Details Design a greeting card congratulating a scientist for using certain traits (curiosity, careful observation, logic, creativity, skepticism, and objectivity) when engaging in a scientific investigation. Be sure to identify how the scientist used each trait in your card.

 Models Make a flow chart in which you describe how scientists develop and evaluate a scientific explanation, including when the data or other piece of evidence do or do not support the explanation.

Scientific Investigations

Mix and Match: *Planning an Investigation*
Mix and match ideas to show what you've learned about methods of scientific investigation.

1. Work on your own, with a partner, or with a small group.

2. Choose three types of scientists from Column A. For each scientist choose one thing to investigate in Column B and one way to conduct the investigation in Column C. Then, on a separate sheet of paper, write and complete the sentence "A _____ is studying ___ using ___" for each of your choices. Provide more details about each investigation, including a possible hypothesis and the independent and dependent variables. Finally, explain why each combination is appropriate.

3. Have your teacher approve your plan.

4. Submit or present your results.

A. Choose Three Types of Scientists	B. Choose One Thing for Each Scientist to Study	C. Choose One Way for Each Scientist to Conduct an Investigation
• geologist • geneticist • biologist • naturalist • astronomer • physicist • food chemist • medical researcher • botanist • volcanologist • paleontologist	___ DNA patterns in mice ___ dinosaur fossils ___ black holes ___ ferret behavior ___ heart disease progression ___ making a faster growing corn plant ___ volcanic layers near Mount St. Helens ___ good sites for oil wells ___ a longer-lasting battery ___ keeping crackers fresh for longer periods of time ___ an energy-efficient location for a new building	___ structured lab experiment ___ observation ___ modeling ___ field observation ___ lab analysis of field samples

Scientific Knowledge

Take Your Pick: *Science and Scientific Knowledge*
Complete the activities to show what you've learned about science and scientific knowledge.

1. Work on your own, with a partner, or with a small group.

2. Choose items below for a total of 10 points. Check your choices.

3. Have your teacher approve your plan.

4. Submit or present your results.

2 Points

_____ **Gathering Evidence** Suppose you are a chemist who is studying the amount of pollutants in your local river. Sketch one way you can collect empirical evidence for your work.

_____ **What Do You Think?** Using a half sheet of paper or an index card, answer these questions: *What was the most interesting fact you learned about science from this lesson? How did studying this lesson change how you thought or felt about learning science?*

5 Points

_____ **You Ask the Questions** Imagine you are tutoring sixth-graders who are studying science. Make up a practice quiz for them about scientific theory and scientific law. Your quiz should be at least five questions long. They can be short-answer, true/false, or multiple choice. Include an answer key.

_____ **A Scientific Skit** Compare a scientific theory, such as the atomic theory or the germ theory, with the use of the word *theory* in a detective or mystery story.

_____ **Defending Review** Imagine you are part of a team of scientists that has done research and published a scientific paper. One of your team members is upset because another group of scientists has criticized your findings. Present a persuasive speech explaining why the scientist should not be upset because peer review and discussion is important to establishing scientific knowledge.

8 Points

_____ **An Empirical Essay** Write a one-page essay that defines and describes empirical evidence. Make sure your essay has an introduction, a body, and a conclusion. Also include some examples of empirical evidence in your essay.

_____ **What's Your Theory?** Research a particular scientific theory. Create a commercial that promotes that theory. In your commercial, explain what a scientific theory is and how it is formed. Also include information about the theory you chose and the research that backs up that theory.

Name _____ Date _____

Science and Society

Take Your Pick: *Science Impacts*
You are a staff member of a science magazine written for children.

1. Work on your own, with a partner, or with a small group.

2. Choose items below for a total of 10 points. Check your choices.

3. Have your teacher approve your plan.

4. Submit or present your results.

2 Points

_____ **In the News** Select a current event about any new development or discovery in science. Write a one-paragraph summary of the development and its importance.

_____ **Time Capsule** Think of five products that were developed using science. Make a timeline to show when each product was created.

_____ **Person on the Street** Do "Person on the Street" interviews of three people about an invention or a recent scientific development. Record each person's response to the question.

5 Points

_____ **Nature Sketch** Make a sketch of a natural environment from your area. Use the sketch as the basis for a poster that will encourage others to practice behaviors that can protect the environment.

_____ **PSA** Create an advertising campaign that includes three ads. Each ad should provide information about a behavior that can help keep individuals healthy. Each ad should include a drawing or photograph to help convey its message.

_____ **Photo Essay** Create a photo essay that contains at least five photographs of subjects from your local area that would appeal to a person with an interest in science. Write a caption for each of your photos.

_____ **10-50-100 Years Ago** Do research to find out about a development in science that was in the news either 10, 50, or 100 years ago. Write a three-paragraph summary that identifies the development, explains why it was important or useful, and describes how or if it is still in use today.

_____ **Invention Poll** Conduct a survey of at least 20 people to find out what they think is the most important invention or scientific development in the last 10 years. Organize the results of the survey in a bar graph.

8 Points

_____ **How's It Work?** Pick a device that was developed using knowledge from science. Develop an illustrated summary that explains how the device works.

_____ **Write a Biography** Write a two-page biography to describe the life and work of any scientist you choose.

Comparing Variables

Purpose A pendulum shows behavior that can be described by observation. Because the pendulum system is subject to error, students can use replication and proper employment of variables to demonstrate how experiments differ from simple observations.

Time Period 1 hour

Preparation Students will need the listed materials and space to conduct the observations.

Teaching Strategies Any mass that swings back and forth exhibits pendulum-like behavior. The students will construct a pendulum and observe its periodicity (time to swing back and forth). Explain to the students that they will then change two system variables: the mass of the pendulum and the length of the string. They will need to distinguish between these independent variables and the controlled variables. Student will need to work in pairs or small groups.

Scoring Rubric

Possible points	Performance indicators
0–10	Appropriate use of materials and equipment
0–30	Accuracy of making observations
0–20	Clarity of recording observations
0–40	Conclusions based on observations

Comparing Variables

Objective

In this activity you will make observations and then perform an experiment to evaluate your observations.

Know the Score!

As you work through this activity, keep in mind that you will be earning a grade for the following:

- how well you work with materials and equipment (10%)
- how accurately you make observations (30%)
- how clearly you record your observations (20%)
- how well you use your knowledge of science to evaluate your observations of the behavior of a pendulum (40%)

Materials and Equipment

- hex nuts, metal (2)
- notebook
- pen
- protractor

- string, 1 meter
- tape
- timer or clock with second hand

Procedure

1. Tape the pen to the side of a table or similar surface, with about half the pen's length lying on the surface.

2. Tie one hex nut to the piece of string. Leave some length at the end to tie on more nuts in later steps.

3. Tie the longer end of the string to the end of the pen so the nut can swing freely.

4. Decide what angle you will use to set the pendulum swinging. Mark it on a suitable surface behind the release point. (Hint: You may need to tape paper underneath the table.)

5. Draw the nut back and release it. As you release, begin the timer. Allow the weight to swing back and forth 5 times. Record the time taken for the 5 swings in the table in step 7.

6. Divide the time by 5 to determine the time for one swing, the period. Record the period in the table.

7. Repeat steps 4 and 5 twice, each time using exactly the same release point. Record your data in the table.

1 MASS	Time (T)	Period (T/5)
Trial 1		
Trial 2		
Trial 3		
Average for three trials		

8. Attach another nut to the end of the string, as close as possible to the first nut. **Don't change the length of string above the nuts.** Repeat Steps 5 to 7. Record your data in the following table.

2 MASSES	Time (T)	Period (T/5)
Trial 1		
Trial 2		
Trial 3		
Average for three trials		

9. Remove one nut. Then shorten the string. Repeat Steps 5 to 7. Be sure to use the same angle when pulling back the string. Record your data in the following table.

SHORT	Time (T)	Period (T/5)
Trial 1		
Trial 2		
Trial 3		
Average for three trials		

10. Lengthen the string so that it is longer than in the first set of trials. Repeat Steps 5 to 7. Be sure to use the same angle when pulling back the string. Record your data in the following table.

LONG	Time (T)	Period (T/5)
Trial 1		
Trial 2		
Trial 3		
Average for three trials		

Analysis

11. What can you conclude about the relationship of mass of the pendulum to the period?

_____

12. What can you conclude about the relationship of length of the pendulum to the period?

_____

_____

13. What other variable in the system could you change? What is the best way to figure out how changing a variable affects the behavior of the pendulum?

_____

_____

Unit 1: The Nature of Science

Vocabulary
Fill in each blank with the term that best completes the following sentences.

1. A(n) _____ is an organized procedure to study something under controlled conditions.

2. A scientific _____ is a well-supported and widely accepted explanation of a natural occurrence.

3. Scientists collect and record _____ .

4. The collective body of observations of a natural phenomenon on which scientific explanations are based is called _____ .

5. A(n) _____ is deliberately changed in a scientific study.

Key Concepts
Read each question below, and circle the best answer.

6. The graph shows the number of a school's male and female athletes.

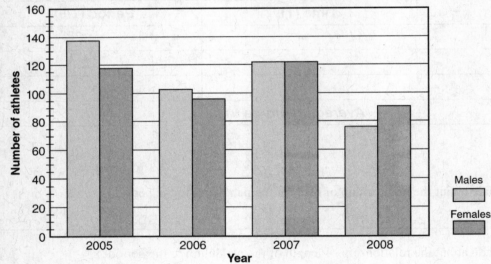

How can the data help the principal increase student participation in athletics?

A. She can identify from the data why students like participating in sports.

B. She can see why there is a decrease in participation between 2005 and 2006.

C. She can tell why there were equal numbers of male and female athletes in 2007.

D. Participation data from the previous year can help her set goals for next year.

7. Laboratory experiments allow scientists to make precise observations. Which one of the following is not a laboratory experiment?

A. counting the population of a country

B. comparing the color of mold in three different Petri dishes

C. measuring how much three plants grow with different amounts of light

D. making observations about the impact of different kinds of fertilizer on seedlings growing near the windows in the lab

8. What is the description of a specific relationship under given conditions in the natural world known as?

A. a tenet of science   C. a theory

B. a scientific law   D. a hypothesis

9. See the drawing of the astrological zodiac signs.

Aquarius	Pisces	Aries	Taurus
Gemini	Cancer	Leo	Virgo
Libra	Scorpio	Sagittarius	Capricorn

Astrology is an example of a pseudoscience. Why is it considered a pseudoscience, unlike astronomy, which is a science?

A. because it is based on the scientific method

B. because it is not based on the scientific method

C. because it can be easily replicated by other scientists

D. because it was a much earlier science

10. Which of the following is not a characteristic of a good scientific investigation?

    A. it can be replicated

    B. it is controlled

    C. it has a large sample size

    D. it has a very small sample size, making it easier for anyone to replicate it

11. Clara tests a hypothesis that the heavier of two materials will insulate cold drinks better than the lighter material. She adds equal volumes of the same cold drink to two different cup types. One cup type is made of a lightweight plastic foam. The other cup type is a heavier, ceramic material. Her sample size is five cups of each material. She records the average of her results in a chart.

Material	Time for liquid to warm to room temperature (hours)
plastic foam	3.25
ceramic	2.50

How are these experimental results valuable to Clara?

    A. The results explain why the materials perform differently.

    B. The results do not support her hypothesis so she should form a new one.

    C. Clara can use a different heavier material to see if she obtains different results.

    D. The results can be communicated with others through newspapers, magazines, and the Internet to increase the validity of her results.

12. After many investigations, Dr. Grossman, a geologist, developed an idea about why certain rocks are found in the Rocky Mountains of North America. Many other geologists accept Dr. Grossman's findings and ideas about why these rock types are present in the Rocky Mountains. What has Dr. Grossman developed?

    A. a law

    B. a theory

    C. a set of facts

    D. a hypothesis

13. Deandra designs an experiment to test how far a rubber band stretches when objects of different mass are suspended from it. She records her data in a chart.

Mass (g)	Stretch (cm)	Mass (g)	Stretch (cm)
10	1	40	4
20	2	50	4.8
30	3	60	5.5

Which variable is independent?

    A. Band type   C. Time

    B. Stretch   D. Mass

Critical Thinking
Answer the following questions in the space provided.

14. Using an example, explain the difference between a hypothesis and a prediction.

_____

_____

_____

_____

_____

15. Evaluate the strengths and limits of science in terms of scope.

_____

_____

_____

_____

Connect ESSENTIAL QUESTIONS

Lessons 1 and 4

Answer the following question in the space provided.

16. Explain how the work of scientists benefits our society as a whole.

_____

_____

_____

_____

_____

Name _____ Date _____

The Nature of Science

Key Concepts
Choose the letter of the best answer.

1. Kathleen made the diagram below to show how scientific knowledge changes over time. Which word or phrase best describes what scientists would do at the point indicated by the blank?

    original idea + new data --> ___?___ --> modified idea

    A. debate the change

    B. change the data

    C. propose a law

    D. form an opinion

2. In which of the following examples would a scale model best be used?

    A. to study organisms under natural conditions

    B. to collect data on different characteristics in a population

    C. to make exact measurements of an object using various pieces of equipment

    D. to develop an explanation for an object that is too large to be studied directly

3. Science affects our lives in different ways. What is one way that science has directly affected our health?

    A. discovery of planets

    B. vaccine development

    C. manufacture of efficient fuels

    D. discovery of the structure of the atom

4. A scientist graphs the mass and volume of three samples, as shown in the graph below.

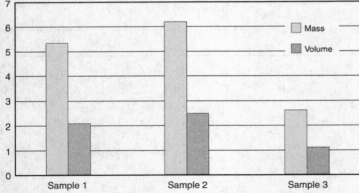

    Which personal trait does the scientist need when attempting to analyze data like the information shown here?

    A. curiosity

    B. imagination

    C. logic

    D. skepticism

5. Sebastian drew a figure to illustrate Boyle's law, which explains the relationship between pressure and volume for a gas kept at constant temperature. His figure looked like the one shown below.

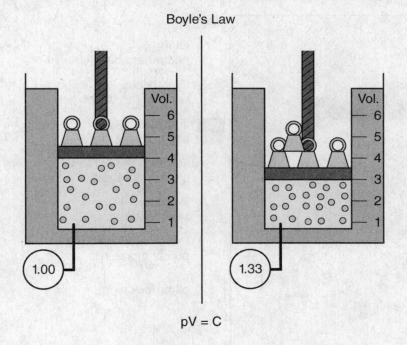

Boyle's Law

$pV = C$

Based on the figure, what happens to a gas due to pressure?

A. The volume of gas increases as pressure decreases, as particles get closer together.

B. The volume of gas decreases as pressure increases, as particles get closer together.

C. The amount of gas increases as pressure decreases.

D. The volume of gas remains constant as pressure increases.

6. Which of the following best supports a scientific explanation?

A. personal bias and the opinion of the scientist

B. an hypothesis formed after initial observations

C. the imagination and originality of the hypothesis

D. experimental data obtained by using technology to make objective measurements

7. Which of the following is a scientific law?

A. Climate is changing due to human activities.

B. Microorganisms are the cause of many illnesses.

C. Tectonic plates move because of a flexible layer beneath Earth.

D. Any two objects exert a gravitational force of attraction on each other.

8. Ricardo was volunteering at a library. The librarian asked him to help clean the research area. Ricardo found the map shown below in a stack of papers.

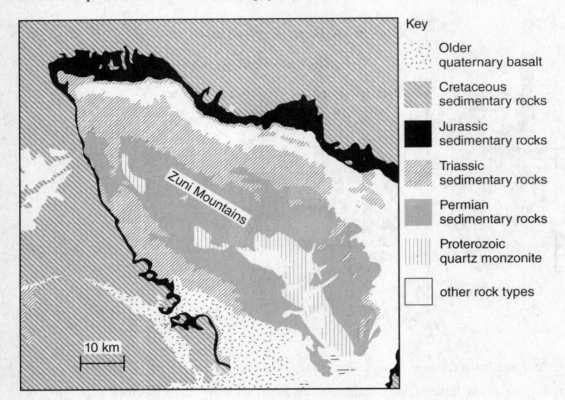

Key

:::: Older quaternary basalt

▨ Cretaceous sedimentary rocks

■ Jurassic sedimentary rocks

⫽ Triassic sedimentary rocks

▦ Permian sedimentary rocks

⫴ Proterozoic quartz monzonite

☐ other rock types

Zuni Mountains

10 km

The librarian told Ricardo that some scientists use a map such as this one. Which type of scientist **most likely** uses this map?

A. chemist

B. biologist

C. geologist

D. physicist

9. There is no single correct way to conduct a scientific investigation. However, there are some techniques that are part of all good investigations. Which of the following is a characteristic of all good scientific investigations?

A. keeping accurate records

B. working with other scientists

C. using expensive scientific equipment

D. conducting the investigation in a laboratory

10. Adam's hypothesis states that an object's speed remains constant over time. Which data supports Adam's hypothesis?

A.

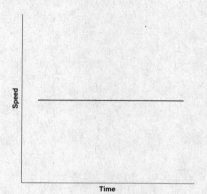

B.

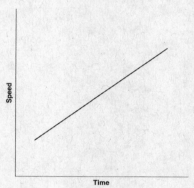

C.

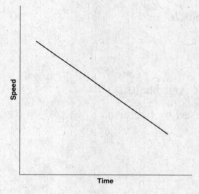

D.

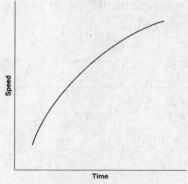

11. Many people need scientific knowledge for their careers. The following image shows an example.

How is this person using scientific knowledge?

A. by planning ahead

B. by developing a hypothesis

C. by taking accurate measurements

D. by using a sturdy table to measure on

12. Which of the following is an example of a pseudoscientific claim?

A. My neighbor and I think that alien radio waves cause cancer.

B. Hundreds of scientists agree that Earth is warming.

C. Numerous experiments have proven that smoking is bad for your health.

D. Many data have been collected that show strep throat is caused by bacteria.

Critical Thinking
Answer the following questions in the space provided.

13. After the results of one experiment, a scientist decides that a long-held scientific theory must be revised. Describe what must be done first before the scientific theory is changed.

_____

_____

_____

Extended Response
Answer the following questions in the space provided.

14. Shakira predicts that hot metal objects do not cool at a constant rate. She experiments by heating a metal object and then allows it to cool to room temperature. She measures the temperature of the metal with a thermometer every half hour, and she carefully records her results in her notebook. From her temperature data, she draws the following graph.

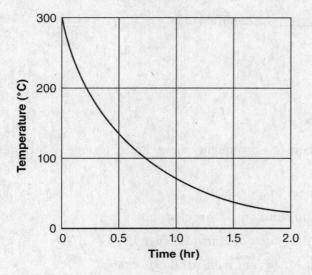

Based on the graph, was Shakira's prediction supported or not supported? Explain how you know.

_____

_____

What could Shakira do to make sure her results are replicable?

_____

_____

Shakira learns that the cooling system turned on approximately one hour after the experiment began. Explain how this could have affected the experiment and what Shakira should do to prevent this from happening in the future.

_____

_____

_____

The Nature of Science

Key Concepts
Choose the letter of the best answer.

1. Kathleen made the diagram below to show how scientific knowledge changes over time. Which word or phrase best describes what scientists would do at the point indicated by the blank?

    original idea + _____?_____ --> modified idea

    A. new evidence

    B. form an opinion

    C. change the data

    D. design an experiment

2. A group of scientists wants to determine how members of a community view climate change. Which of the following would best accomplish this goal?

    A. creating a model of the effects of climate change on an ecosystem

    B. taking a survey of a group of people about their opinions on climate change

    C. performing a laboratory experiment to replicate the effects of climate change

    D. conducting fieldwork to analyze the different gases that contribute to climate change

3. What is one way that science has directly affected our ease of travel?

    A. discovery of planets

    B. vaccine development

    C. development of the airplane

    D. discovery of the structure of the atom

4. A scientist measures the mass and volume of three samples, then plots the data on the graph below.

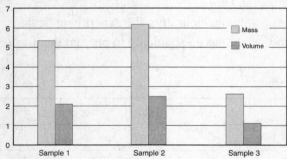

    Which personal trait does a scientist require when collecting data and making measurements like those recorded on this graph?

    A. curiosity

    B. creativity

    C. logic

    D. objectivity

5. The figure below illustrates Boyle's law, which describes the effect of pressure on the volume of a gas that is kept at constant temperature.

Boyle's Law

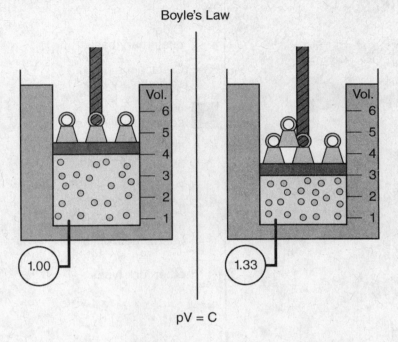

$pV = C$

Based on the figure, which of these statements is an accurate explanation of Boyle's law?

A. Boyle's law explains why the volume of a gas gets smaller when the pressure on a gas is increases.

B. Boyle's law explains what happens to a gas if the temperature of the gas is changed.

C. Boyle's law identifies the relationships among temperature, pressure, and volume for gases in a closed system.

D. Boyle's law states that, as the pressure on a certain amount of gas increases, its volume decreases.

6. Which phrase defines the limits of what science can study?

A. any phenomenon that a scientist can observe or model

B. only a phenomenon that a scientist can observe with instruments

C. only a phenomenon that a scientist can observe without instruments

D. only a phenomenon that a scientist will be able to explain with certainty

7. What term best describes the following statement?

"Any two objects exert a gravitational force of attraction on each other."

A. a scientific law

B. a scientific theory

C. a scientific hypothesis

D. a scientific observation

8. Examine the map shown in the figure below.

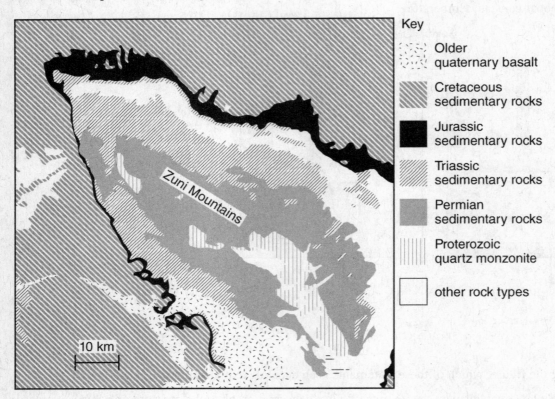

Key

░ Older quaternary basalt

▨ Cretaceous sedimentary rocks

■ Jurassic sedimentary rocks

▨ Triassic sedimentary rocks

▨ Permian sedimentary rocks

▦ Proterozoic quartz monzonite

☐ other rock types

Some of the information used to create the map was most likely gathered during what type of investigations?

A. fieldwork by geologist working in the area

B. biologists observing the animals in the area

C. laboratory experiments done far away from the area

D. surveys of people living in the area

9. There is no single way to conduct a scientific investigation. However, there are some techniques that are part of all good investigations. Which of the following is a characteristic of a poor scientific investigation?

A. A large sample size is used.

B. The results cannot be replicated.

C. The scientist keeps accurate records.

D. Repeated trials have been conducted.

10. Adam's hypothesis states that an object's speed constantly changes. Which data requires Adam to form a new hypothesis?

A.

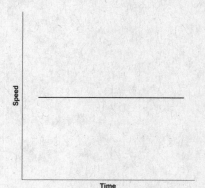

B.

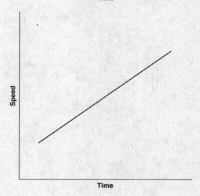

C.

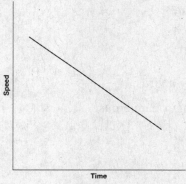

D.

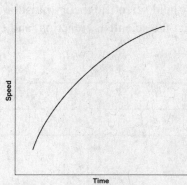

11. Many people need scientific knowledge for their careers. The following image shows an example.

How is this person using scientific knowledge?

A. by planning ahead

B. by using the proper tools

C. by taking the time to avoid mistakes

D. by using the metric system when measuring

12. Which of the following is an example of a pseudoscientific claim?

A. Hundreds of scientists agree that Earth is warming.

B. Many people believe that aliens built the pyramids.

C. Many data have been collected that show the flu is caused by a virus.

D. Numerous experiments have shown that driving while texting is dangerous.

Critical Thinking

Answer the following questions in the space provided.

13. After the results of an experiment, a scientist decides that a long-held scientific theory must be revised. The scientist modifies the theory and tells other scientists. Predict the scientists' reaction, and explain why they might react that way.

_____

_____

_____

Extended Response

Answer the following questions in the space provided.

14. Shakira predicts that hot metal objects cool at constant rates. She experiments by heating a metal object with a Bunsen burner and then allowing it to cool to room temperature. She measures the temperature of the metal every half hour, and she carefully records her results in her notebook. From her temperature data, she draws the following graph.

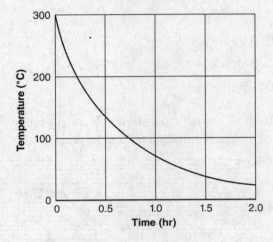

What tool should Shakira use to collect quantitative data during her experiment?

_____

Based on the graph, was Shakira's prediction supported or not supported? Explain how you know.

_____

_____

What could Shakira do to make sure her results are replicable?

_____

_____

Shakira learns that the heating and air conditioning system turned on at around one hour after the experiment began. Explain whether this could affect the experiment and what Shakira should do.

_____

_____

_____

Name _____ Date _____

Measurement and Data

Choose the letter of the best answer.

1. Below is an example of a model.

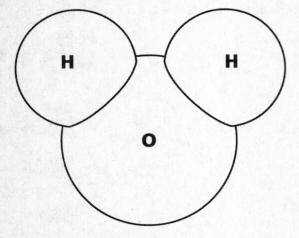

   What would this model be used to study?

   A. an atom

   B. a neutron

   C. a molecule

   D. a DNA strand

2. What is the term for the way scientists use only a few numbers to represent a very large or very small number?

   A. metric units

   B. measurements

   C. scientific notation

   D. customary system of units

3. According to Thomas Malthus, human population grows much faster than the production of food increases. What type of model would best represent this scenario?

   A. a scale model

   B. a physical model

   C. a conceptual model

   D. a mathematical model

4. What would scientists in 2010 most likely have used to project levels of atmospheric carbon dioxide between the years 2011 and 2100?

   A. a model

   B. a prototype

   C. a simulation

   D. a probeware

5. The line graph below shows the average annual salary at a company over a nine-year period.

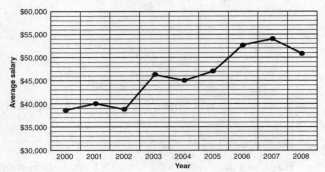

   How much **greater** was the average salary in 2007 than in 2008?

   A. $2,600

   B. $3,000

   C. $3,800

   D. $4,400

6. A laboratory scientist wants to heat a liquid substance and then store it in several containers. What tools would the scientist most likely use?

   A. hot plate and test tubes

   B. stopwatch and beakers

   C. thermometer and graduated cylinders

   D. Bunsen burner and triple beam balances

7. The school physician performed an experiment to investigate the effects of aerobic exercise on high school freshmen. He examined 25 student volunteers and found them to be in good health. He then had the students perform aerobic exercises, such as jogging, swimming, and bicycling. The doctor recorded the students' pulse rates before each activity, during each activity, and after each activity. Which was the dependent variable in this experiment?

A. the physician

B. the exercises

C. the volunteers

D. the pulse rates

8. Which measurement and SI unit are incorrectly matched?

A. length: feet

B. time: second

C. mass: kilogram

D. temperature: Kelvin

9. What type of model often looks like, acts like, and copies the structure of the object it represents?

A. a simulation

B. a physical model

C. a conceptual model

D. a mathematical model

10. The image below shows a type of model used by scientists.

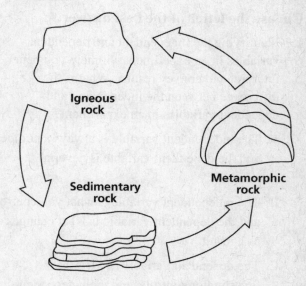

What type of model is shown in this image?

A. a scale model

B. a physical model

C. a conceptual model

D. a mathematical model

Representing Data

Choose the letter of the best answer.

1. Identifying the independent and dependent variables in an experiment will help you better interpret and convey results. What is the difference between the independent and dependent variables in an experiment?

   A. The independent variable is always a number, and the dependent variable is never a number.

   B. The independent variable is what you control, and the dependent variable is what changes as a result.

   C. The dependent variable is what the investigator controls, and the independent variable is what happens as a result of this.

   D. The dependent variable is typically found in the first column of a table, and the independent variable is typically found in the second column.

2. Which of the following is a limitation of using a model to study something?

   A. A model cannot represent a thing exactly.

   B. A model cannot help study things that are dangerous.

   C. A model cannot reproduce things that are too far away.

   D. A model cannot show things that are too small or too large.

3. Scientists often use visual or mathematical representations to investigate items that are very large, very small, or otherwise difficult to study. What are these visual or mathematical representations called?

   A. experiments

   B. hypotheses

   C. models

   D. observations

4. A graph can help scientists display and convey data. What part of a line graph shows trends?

   A. title

   B. legend

   C. *x*- and *y*-axis labels

   D. line of best fit

5. The pie graph below shows the distribution of grades on a test taken in Dr. Kurilla's class.

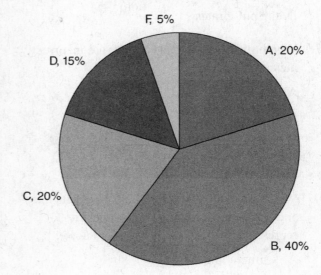

If 20 students took the test, how many students earned a grade of B or better?

   A. 9 students

   B. 12 students

   C. 15 students

   D. 18 students

Scientific Tools and Measurement

Choose the letter of the best answer.

1. A scientist wants to track a hurricane and predict where it will go next. What is the best tool for the scientist to use?

   A. a computer

   B. a hand lens

   C. an electron microscope

   D. a magnetic resonance image

2. Which of the following is the most likely reason why scientists use approximate measurements?

   A. Scientists do not use approximate measurements as that would be unscientific.

   B. Scientists use approximate measurements to determine whether the data they collected is reasonable.

   C. Scientists use approximate measurements to record images of objects or environments in a brief interval of time.

   D. Scientists use approximate measurements to help take measurements that cannot be detected by the senses alone.

3. Why was the International System of Units (SI) developed?

   A. It was developed to compete with the English Standard System of Units.

   B. It was developed to allow countries to follow their own systems of measurement.

   C. It was developed to help scientists keep their data, observations, and measurements secret from other scientists.

   D. It was developed to help scientists compare measurements made by different people in different locations using different tools.

4. The image below shows four measurements (small dots) and an actual value (larger center).

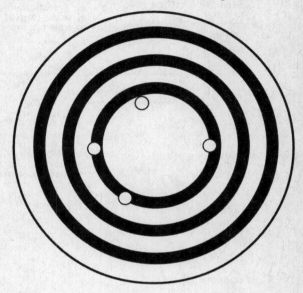

   How can we describe these measurements in terms of accuracy and precision?

   A. The measurements are accurate but not precise.

   B. The measurements are precise but not accurate.

   C. The measurements are both accurate and precise.

   D. The measurements are neither accurate nor precise.

5. You are making a measurement using meters and find that the number value is 10. What is the correct way to write this scientific measurement?

   A. meters

   B. 10

   C. 10 meters

   D. meters 10

Lesson Quiz

Models and Simulations

Choose the letter of the best answer.

1. The image below shows a model.

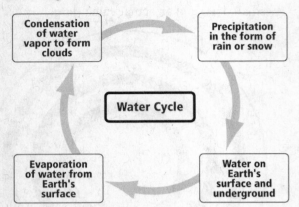

What type of model is shown in this image?

A. a scale model

B. a physical model

C. a conceptual model

D. a mathematical model

2. A scientist wants to see what would happen if a truck's tires slipped on ice. What would the scientist use to test how the truck's tires would function in this example?

A. a system

B. a simulation

C. a conceptual model

D. a mathematical model

3. Which of the following is not an example of a physical model?

A. a toy car

B. a miniature train

C. a stuffed animal

D. a chemical equation

4. Which of the following best describes a typical disadvantage of using a mathematical model?

A. A mathematical model may be too dangerous or too expensive to study.

B. A mathematical model may not behave exactly like the object it represents.

C. A mathematical model may not be able to include certain ideas, which may lead to misconceptions about the system.

D. A mathematical model may not include all the data, variables, and factors that lead to understanding a system or process fully.

5. What kind of model allows a scientist to understand a large object by studying the object at a smaller size?

A. a simulation

B. a scale model

C. a conceptual model

D. a mathematical model

Representing Data

Climb the Pyramid: *Represent Data Three Ways*
Climb the pyramid to show what you have learned about representing data.

1. Work on your own, with a partner, or with a small group.

2. Choose one item from each layer of the pyramid. Check your choices.

3. Have your teacher approve your plan.

4. Submit or present your results.

__ Model

Make a model of your classroom. The model can be two-dimensional like a map or scale drawing, or it can be three-dimensional. Present your model to the class and list at least two advantages and two limitations of your model.

__ Table 1

Toss a coin 100 times and make a table that shows how many tosses were heads and how many were tails. If you were to graph these data, how might you show your results?

__ Table 2

Make a table that shows how many students in the classroom write with either their right hand or their left hand. If you wanted to visualize these data, what would be a good way to show your results?

__ Graph 1

Choose a location and find out the average temperature it experiences each month for a year. Make a line graph to present your data. Which month is the hottest? Which month is the coolest?

__ Graph 2

Make a line graph that shows a car traveling 80 kilometers per hour for 400 kilometers. Approximately how long would it take the car to travel 360 kilometers?

__ Graph 3

Make a line graph that shows how the average size of the ozone hole over the South Pole has changed between the years 1979 to 1994.

Data:

1981 (0.5 million square kilometers), 1982 (3), 1983 (7), 1984 (9), 1985 (14), 1986 (10), 1987 (19), 1988 (8), 1989 (19), 1990 (18), 1991 (19), 1992 (21), 1993 (22), 1994 (23)

What overall trend do you see in your graph? How would you explain data that do not fit the trend?

Scientific Tools and Measurement

Climb the Pyramid: *Accuracy of Measurements*

1. Work on your own, with a partner, or with a small group.

2. Choose one item from each layer of the pyramid. Check your choices.

3. Have your teacher approve your plan.

4. Submit or present your results.

__ Proper Tools

Write several sentences to answer the following questions: Why is it important to choose proper tools and to use them correctly in science? What are some reasons why data might be inaccurate?

__ Conversion Factors

Pick an object to use as a unit of measure, such as a pencil. Measure the width of your desk with this unit. Use a meter stick to determine the exact length of your object. Measure your desk again with the meter stick. Compare the measurements made with your chosen unit and with the meter stick.

__ Design an Experiment

Design an experiment to test an hypothesis. Write the steps that you will follow. List the tools that you will need to perform the experiment. Explain how each tool will be used. With your teacher's permission, follow the steps to conduct the experiment. Record your results.

__ Measurement Standards

Write a skit that portrays a conversation between scientists. The dialogue must include an explanation of why the International System of Units (SI) was developed and describe some of the advantages of using the SI.

__ Measuring Length, Mass, Time, and Temperature

Make a matching worksheet to review the following: types of measurement including length, mass, time, and temperature; their SI base units; and a tool used to measure each.

__ Scientific Tools

Write a short, newspaper-style article that answers the following question: How are computers and technology used as tools for scientific investigations?

Name _____ Date _____

Unit 2 Lesson 3

Models and Simulations

Alternative Assessment

Mix and Match: *Model Analysis*

Mix and match ideas to show what you've learned about models and simulations.

1. Work on your own, with a partner, or with a small group.

2. Choose one information source from Column A, two ways to analyze the model from Column B, and one option from Column C. Check your choices.

3. Have your teacher approve your plan.

4. Submit or present your results.

A. Choose One Information Source	B. Choose Two Things to Analyze	C. Choose One Way to Communicate Analysis
___ a physical model ___ a picture or description of a physical model ___ a mathematical model ___ a conceptual model _____	___ the specific advantages and limitations of the model ___ how the model can be used to make predictions ___ a detailed description of the types of simulations the model could be utilized in ___ a comparison of the model to the actual object, system, or process it represents ___ an explanation about what features make the model a physical, mathematical, or conceptual model	___ poster with both text and illustrations ___ multimedia presentation ___ oral report ___ written report _____

Advantages of the Metric System as Way to Measure

Purpose The students will develop their own system of measurement and then use the metric system as a comparison to determine which is better. The aim of the assessment is to evaluate the students' understanding of the advantages of the metric system as a way to measure the world around us. It also tests students' ability to convert between different metric units.

Time Period 1 hour

Preparation Students will need the listed materials and space to conduct the observations. Students will need items to measure length in metric units and will create their own measurement device. Students will need appropriate objects to derive their own units of measurement.

Teaching Strategies The students will make their own units using the paper clip and pencil as standards. They will derive the conversion factor to convert "pencils" into "paper clips." This will be an arbitrary quantity, such as 4.5 paper clips = 1 pencil. They will use two strips of masking tape stuck together to make their own tape measure in "paper clip" units. They will use this to measure a specified set of 10 objects around the classroom. Then they will convert the size of each object from the "paper clip" unit into the "pencil" unit (no calculator allowed). This procedure is timed. The measurement is repeated with the same 10 objects, using the metric tape measure. This time students convert from centimeters into meters. Again the procedure is timed. The time for the two procedures is compared. Since conversion is easier using metric units, it will be faster than with the arbitrary invented units. This activity works best when students work in pairs.

Scoring Rubric

Possible points	Performance indicators
0–30	Appropriate use of materials and equipment
0–20	Accuracy of making observations
0–20	Clarity of recording observations
0–30	Conclusions based on observations

Advantages of the Metric System as Way to Measure

Objective

You have learned about the metric system and how to convert between units. In this activity, you will derive your own system of measurement and evaluate how well it works compared to the metric system.

Know the Score!

As you work through this activity, keep in mind that you will be earning a grade for the following:

- how well you work with materials and equipment (30%)

- how accurately you make observations (20%)

- how clearly you record your observations (20%)

- how well you use your knowledge of the metric system to compare with your own system of measurement (30%)

Materials and Equipment

- marker pen
- masking tape
- metric tape measure
- paper clip

- paper
- pencil
- timer

Procedure

1. Place the pencil on the piece of paper.

2. Mark each end of the pencil on the piece of paper. This length represents your "pencil" unit of measurement.

3. On one of the marks, place the paper clip so it is aligned with the other mark. Mark the end of the paper clip. Place the paper clip on this new mark and again mark the end. Count the number of times the paper clip marks fit into the marks that indicate the length of the pencil. It's okay if it's not an exact number. The number of paper clip lengths it takes to make one pencil length is your conversion factor. Write the conversion factor below.

_____

4. Take a length of masking tape, about as long as your arm. The exact length is not important. Take another piece of masking tape about the same length as the first. Apply these two pieces with the sticky sides together to make a single length of masking tape.

5. Use the pencil that you used in step 1 to mark units of "paper clip" on the masking tape. You can now use the masking tape as a tape measure in "paper clip" units.

6. Select 10 objects around the room, such as pieces of furniture, the side of a picture, and so on. Record each of these in the table provided.

7. Begin measuring the objects and enter the measurements in the table.

Object	Paper clip units	Pencil units*	Centimeters	Meters*

*Calculate using conversion factor

8. When you are finished, perform the conversion of "paper clips" units into "pencils." Do NOT use a calculator to do this. Use the timer to time how long it takes to complete all your calculations. Write the time taken below.

_____

9. Using the metric tape measure, measure the same 10 objects in centimeters. Enter the measurements in the table.

10. Now convert your centimeter measurements into meters. Again, do NOT use a calculator to do this. Again, use the timer to time how long it takes to complete all your calculations. Write the time taken below.

_____

Analysis

11. Which measurement system took longer to convert measurements?

_____

_____

12. Why did it take you longer to use one system compared with the other?

_____

_____

13. What can you conclude about metric units as a measurement system compared with the one you created?

_____

_____

_____

Unit 2: Measurement and Data

Vocabulary

Fill in each blank with the term that best completes the following sentences.

1. Visual or mathematical representations used to develop scientific explanations are called _____ .

2. A _____ is a description of something that includes a number and a unit.

3. A toy car is an example of a _____ that represents a real car.

4. The data for the _____ are usually found in the first column of a data table.

5. Scientists use to _____ understand how systems work.

Key Concepts

Read each question below, and circle the best answer.

6. This line graph shows a company's average annual salary over nine years.

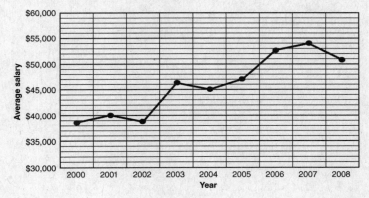

From 2000 to 2008, how many times did the average annual salary decrease?

A. once

B. twice

C. three times

D. four times

7. Mrs. Rehak shows her students a model of the three states of matter.

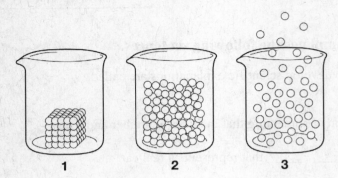

1   2   3

Which part(s) of Mrs. Rehak's model represents a gas?

A. 1 and 2   C. 2

B. 3   D. 1

8. Scientists use which one of the following units to measure mass?

    A. pounds   C. kilograms

    B. meters   D. ounces

9. Which is a tool that scientists would not likely use in a lab?

    A. test tube   C. electron microscope

    B. hot plate   D. yard stick

10. How should scientists express very large numbers when reporting data?

    A. in scientific notation

    B. to the tenth decimal point

    C. as a fraction

    D. in inches

11. Scientists use models and simulations in their work. Which one of the following does a simulation not do?

    A. imitates the function of the thing it represents

    B. imitates the behavior of the thing it represents

    C. imitates the process of the thing it represents

    D. takes the place of the thing it represents

Name _____ Date _____

12. Look at the diagram below of the rock cycle.

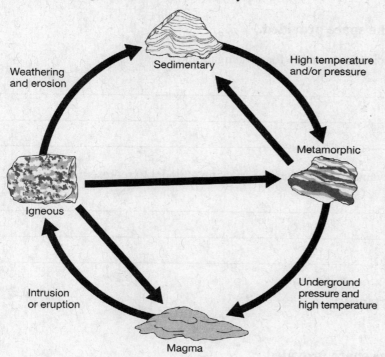

What does the diagram represent?

A. mathematical model

B. simulation

C. conceptual model

D. physical model

13. Emmanuel compared the growth of plants in full sun and part shade.

Plant Growth

Conditions	Initial height (cm)	Height after 10 days (cm)	Height after 20 days (cm)	Height after 30 days (cm)
Full sun	20	24	27	31
Part shade	20	22	23	25

Emmanuel decides to create a line graph to show the growth of the plant grown in full sun. What would be the correct labels for the axes of the line graph?

A. Full sun and Number of days

B. Height (cm) and Conditions

C. Conditions and Number of days

D. Number of days and Height (cm)

Critical Thinking
Answer the following questions in the space provided.

14. What advantage do computers give scientists as tools for investigations?

_____

_____

_____

15. Explain what a model is. What disadvantage could there be in using a model to represent data?

_____

_____

_____

Connect ESSENTIAL QUESTIONS

Lessons 1 and 3

Answer the following question in the space provided.

16. Define mathematical model and conceptual model. Give at least one example of each. What kind of data would each represent?

_____

_____

_____

_____

_____

Measurement and Data

Key Concepts
Choose the letter of the best answer.

1. Earth has a mass of 5.9736 x 10²⁴ kilograms. What is this number in regular (not scientific) notation?

   A. 59,736,000,000,000

   B. 59,736,000,000,000,000,000

   C. 5,973,600,000,000,000,000,000,000

   D. 5,973,600,000,000,000,000,000,000,000

2. What scientific tool would best be used to study your cheek cells?

   A. a hand lens

   B. an electron microscope

   C. an MRI (magnetic resonance imagery)

   D. a CAT scan (computerized axial tomography)

3. Wilson measured the air temperature at a particular location every three hours for one day. He organized his findings using a bar graph.

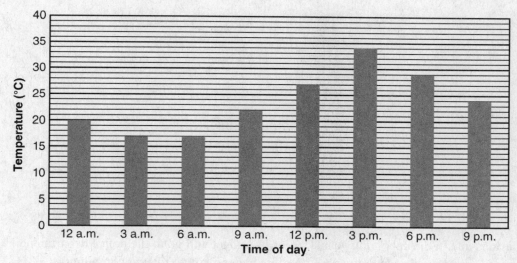

   At what time was the temperature the **hottest**?

   A. 12:00 p.m. (noon)

   B. 3:00 p.m.

   C. 6:00 p.m.

   D. 9:00 p.m.

4. The students in Mrs. Dhaibar's science class take a test. The results of the test are shown in the table below.

Grade	Percentage of students who earned this grade
A	25%
B	25%
C	35%
D	10%
F	5%

Mrs. Dhaibar creates a pie chart to display this data.

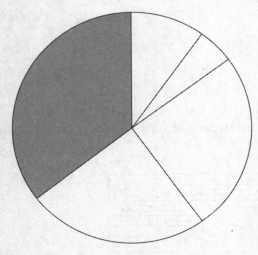

Which grade does the shaded region correspond to?

A. A

B. B

C. C

D. D

5. A city council decides that in the upcoming year, 15% of its budget will go to the police department, 10% of its budget will go to the fire department, 30% of its budget will go toward community development, 20% of its budget will go toward public works, and 25% of its budget will go toward various government operations. Which of the following graphs would most effectively represent this data?

A. line graph

B. scatter plot

C. circle graph

D. box-and-whisker plot

6. Which of the following is not a correct match between a measurement and the tool used to make that measurement?

   A. time: stopwatch

   B. length: meter stick

   C. mass: graduated cylinder

   D. temperature: thermometer

7. A biologist uses a model of a cell to teach a class about the different parts that make up a cell. What is the most likely reason the biologist chose a model instead of an actual cell to teach the class?

   A. A real cell is too large to study.

   B. A real cell is too small to study.

   C. A real cell is too far away to study.

   D. A real cell is too dangerous to study.

8. Scientists are conducting an experiment in which they give people different amounts of Vitamin C to determine whether Vitamin C intake has an effect on how often a person gets sick. What is the dependent variable in this experiment?

   A. the amount of vitamin C

   B. the type of illness a person gets

   C. the brand of vitamin C being used

   D. the number of illnesses a person gets

9. The executive board of a technological company wants to show the monetary budget for each of the departments of the company. What type of model would best be used in this example?

   A. a scale model

   B. a physical model

   C. a conceptual model

   D. a mathematical model

10. Below are the results of a chemistry lab experiment.

Trial #	Measurement (kg)
1	35
2	36
3	34
4	36
5	35

If the actual value were 35 kg, what can be said about the measurements?

A. The measurements are accurate and precise.

B. The measurements are accurate but not precise.

C. The measurements are precise but not accurate.

D. The measurements are neither accurate nor precise.

11. A graphic designer shows her plans for a new shopping mall by using a scale model of the actual mall. Why did the graphic designer most likely use a scale model and not another type of model?

A. She used a scale model because she wanted to show quantitative situations of shops.

B. She used a scale model because she wanted to show something that is too large to see.

C. She used a scale model because she wanted to show the patterns of behavior of shoppers.

D. She used a scale model because she wanted to show a process that cannot be copied in real life.

12. How is a physical model most limited in its use?

A. It is limited by the existing data and variables.

B. It is limited by ideas that can cause misconceptions.

C. It is limited by the exclusion of factors that are important.

D. It is limited by the model not behaving like the object it represents.

Critical Thinking

Answer the following questions in the space provided.

13. Below are two models of our solar system: the geocentric model on the left and the heliocentric model on the right.

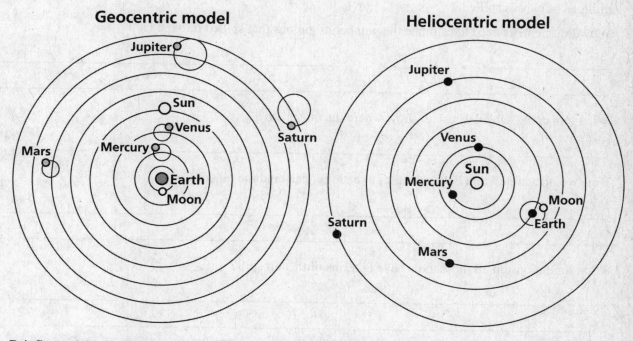

Geocentric model   **Heliocentric model**

Briefly explain the differences between how the geocentric model and the heliocentric model explain the solar system.

_____

_____

_____

Extended Response
Answer the following questions in the space provided.

14. Scientists are unsure exactly how much oil spilled into the Gulf of Mexico when an oil rig exploded in 2010. Some scientists estimated that thousands of barrels spilled, and some scientists estimated that millions of barrels spilled.

   Why did scientists need to estimate the number of gallons that spilled into the Gulf?

   _____

   _____

   What tool could scientists use to show where the oil spread?

   _____

   How would a simulation help scientists to better understand the oil spill?

   _____

   _____

   What limitations do all these tools have in terms of this oil spill?

   _____

   _____

Measurement and Data

Key Concepts
Choose the letter of the best answer.

1. Earth has a mass of 5,973,600,000,000,000,000,000,000 kilograms. How is this written in scientific notation?

   A. $5.9736 \; ? \; 10^{24}$ kg

   B. $597.36 \; ? \; 10^{22}$ kg

   C. $59,736 \; ? \; 10^{25}$ kg

   D. 5,973,600,000,000,000,000,000,000 kg

2. What scientific tool would best be used to compare the masses of two rocks?

   A. a hot plate

   B. a test tube

   C. an electronic balance

   D. an electron microscope

3. Wilson measured the air temperature at a particular location every three hours for one day. He organized his findings using a bar graph.

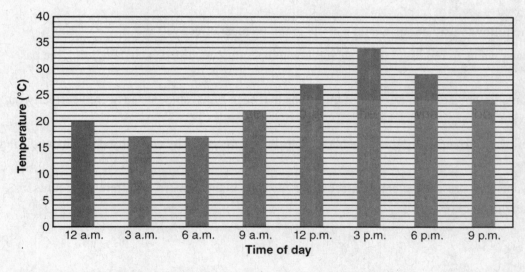

   What is the difference between the coldest and the warmest temperatures on this day?

   A. 7 °C

   B. 11 °C

   C. 13 °C

   D. 17 °C

4. The students in Mrs. Dhaibar's science class take a test. She uses a circle graph to show the results of the test. Each wedge shows a grade range. For example, one wedge shows how many students earned an A.

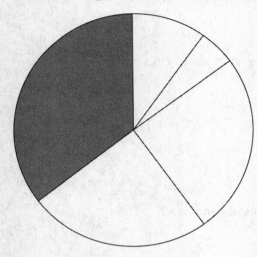

Which percentage of students got the grade shown in the shaded wedge?

A. 15%

B. 25%

C. 35%

D. 50%

5. For which of the following situations would a circle graph be most effective?

A. a meteorologist wants to represent the high and low temperature recorded each day during the past month

B. a teacher wants to represent the number of questions that each of his students answered correctly on their final exam

C. a city council wants to represent the percentage of its budget received by each city department during the past year

D. a scientist wants to represent the height reached by each pea plant exposed to different amounts of carbon dioxide in an experiment

6. Which of the following is not a correct match between a measurement and the tool used to make that measurement?

   A. length: meter stick

   B. time: graduated cylinder

   C. temperature: thermometer

   D. mass: triple beam balance

7. A scientist is using a model to predict when a volcano might erupt again. What kind of model is the scientist most likely to use?

   A. scale model

   B. computer model

   C. physical model

   D. diagram

8. Scientists are conducting an experiment in which they give people different amounts of Vitamin C to determine whether Vitamin C intake has an effect on how often a person gets sick. What is the independent variable in this experiment?

   A. the amount of vitamin C

   B. how often a person gets sick

   C. the type of illness a person gets

   D. the brand of vitamin C being used

9. The executive board of a technological company wants to illustrate the task list for each of the different departments that make up the company. What type of model would best be used in this example?

   A. a scale model

   B. a physical model

   C. a conceptual model

   D. a mathematical model

10. Below are the results of a chemistry lab experiment.

Trial #	Measurement (kg)
1	35
2	36
3	34
4	36
5	35

If the actual value was 42 kg, what can be said about the measurements?

A. The measurements are accurate and precise.

B. The measurements are accurate but not precise.

C. The measurements are precise but not accurate.

D. The measurements are neither accurate nor precise.

11. A manager shows her plans for organizing the flow of information through a workplace using a conceptual model. Why did the manager most likely use a conceptual model and not another type of model?

A. She used a conceptual model because she wanted to show something that is too large to see.

B. She used a conceptual model because she wanted to show patterns of behavior of people.

C. She used a conceptual model because she wanted to show the layout of offices in the workplace.

D. She used a conceptual model because she wanted to show a process that cannot be studied directly.

12. How is a mathematical model most limited in its use?

A. It is limited by the existing data and variables.

B. It is limited by ideas that can cause misconceptions.

C. It is limited by the size of the object that is being modeled.

D. It is limited by the model not behaving like the object it represents.

Critical Thinking

Answer the following questions in the space provided.

13. Below are two models of our solar system: the geocentric model on the left and the heliocentric model on the right.

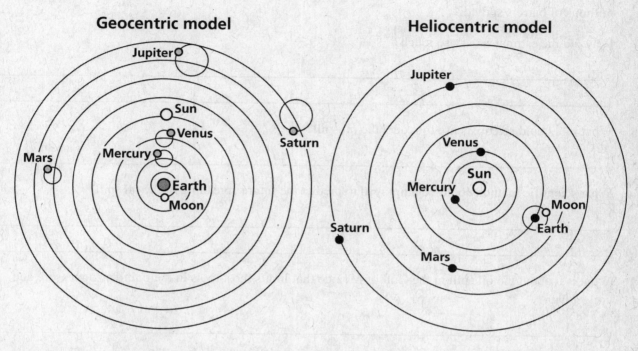

Compare these two models. Briefly explain why scientists rejected one model in favor of the other model.

_____

_____

_____

Extended Response
Answer the following questions in the space provided.

14. Scientists are unsure exactly how much oil spilled into the Gulf of Mexico when an oil rig exploded in 2010. Some scientists estimated that thousands of barrels spilled, and some scientists estimated that millions of barrels spilled.

    Why did the estimates vary so much?

    _____

    _____

    What tool could scientists use to model the oil spill?

    _____

    What scientific method could be employed to predict the future spreading of the oil spill?

    _____

    _____

    What is it about the oil spill in the Gulf of Mexico that limits most tools in their ability to measure and collect data?

    _____

    _____

Engineering, Technology and Society

Choose the letter of the best answer.

1. Plastic is made up of large molecules; it is flexible and has low density and low conductivity. What type of material is plastic?

   A. a metal

   B. a ceramic

   C. a polymer

   D. a semiconductor

2. Jacob is trying to figure out whether to drive, ride a bike, or just walk to school for his freshman year of college. He wants to create a table that shows cost, efficiency, speed, ease of storage, and emissions of the three options. What can he use to determine the best choice?

   A. a system

   B. a prototype

   C. a Pugh chart

   D. a trade-off table

3. Two scientists are shown with a test model of a new design.

   What step in the engineering design process may not yet have been completed by these scientists?

   A. identify a need

   B. build a prototype

   C. communicate results

   D. brainstorm a solution

4. Which disciplines do engineers most use to solve real-world problems?

   A. biology, chemistry, and physics

   B. technology, science, and mathematics

   C. psychology, sociology, and mass communications

   D. history, geology, and physics

5. Bacteria is often used to treat wastewater. This is an example of which of the following?

   A. a new technology developed from a living organism

   B. a living organism used as part of a technological application

   C. making a new organism through the use of technology

   D. a technology applied to a living organism to help it with life processes

6. The diagram shows a possible effect of climate change.

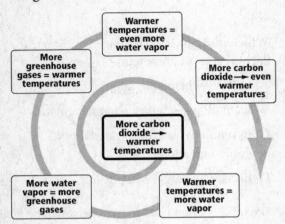

According to this diagram, what best describes the cycle of events resulting from an increase of carbon dioxide?

A. a manual control

B. a positive feedback loop

C. a negative feedback loop

D. an automatic control system

7. A student is trying to measure a wooden board for a class project. What type of tool best meets the student's needs?

A. a cyber tool

B. a complex tool

C. a physical tool

D. a composite tool

8. Technology has many effects. What type of effect is most desirable?

A. expected favorable

B. expected unfavorable

C. unexpected favorable

D. unexpected unfavorable

9. The image below shows a common city scene.

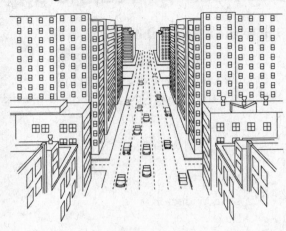

What does this image best represent?

A. the natural world

B. the designed world

C. the scientific world

D. the mechanical world

10. Authorities in a certain country where high population growth rates are considered normal decided not to participate in a polio vaccine program because they believed the vaccine was designed to slow population growth in that country. Which of the following factors most directly contributed to this decision?

A. culture

B. economics

C. technology

D. environment

The Engineering Design Process

Choose the letter of the best answer.

1. Which of the following is not a skill an engineer would use to design a bridge?

    A. creative thinking

    B. methodical thinking

    C. using math and models

    D. designing a controlled experiment

2. What is the correct order of steps to follow in the engineering design process?

    A. report the results; identify a need; carry out research and brainstorm solutions; build and test a prototype

    B. identify a need; carry out research and brainstorm solutions; build and test a prototype; report the results

    C. build and test a prototype; report the results; identify a need; carry out research and brainstorm solutions

    D. carry out research and brainstorm solutions; build and test a prototype; report the results; identify a need

3. An engineer is designing a robot. The engineer builds the first robot to test and troubleshoot problems for future robots. What is the first test robot called?

    A. a model

    B. a prototype

    C. a computer

    D. an application

4. Which of the following is the best definition of engineering?

    A. the study of the natural world

    B. the application of science for practical purposes

    C. the application of science and mathematics to solve real-life problems

    D. the use of tools, machines, materials, and processes to meet human needs

5. The Venn diagram below shows the relationship between science, technology, mathematics, and engineering.

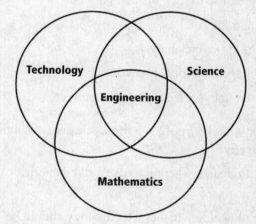

According to this diagram, which statement best describes this relationship?

    A. Engineering uses only science and technology to solve problems.

    B. Engineering uses only science and mathematics to solve problems.

    C. Engineering uses only mathematics and technology to solve problems.

    D. Engineering uses science, mathematics, and technology to solve problems.

Methods of Analysis

Lesson Quiz

Choose the letter of the best answer.

1. A company deciding whether to adopt a new technology conducts a risk-benefit analysis. Which of the following outcomes of the analysis would most likely convince the company to adopt the technology?

   A. The benefits outweigh the risks.

   B. The risks outweigh the benefits.

   C. Adopting the technology leads to risks.

   D. Adopting the technology leads to benefits.

2. A person shopping for a new cell phone decides to buy the model with a longer battery life but with less data storage. What method did the person use to pick the cell phone?

   A. a trade-off

   B. a life-cycle analysis

   C. a technological breakthrough

   D. an unexpected unfavorable effect

3. For which purpose is a life-cycle analysis most effective?

   A. to decide whether to use a risk-benefit analysis

   B. to decide whether a technology should be tested

   C. to analyze the features of a product compared with other products

   D. to figure out the total cost of producing, using, and disposing of technology.

4. A fire-proof robot prototype is being tested when it short circuits and, to the surprise of the researchers, catches fire. What kind of effect has just happened?

   A. an expected favorable effect

   B. an unexpected favorable effect

   C. an expected unfavorable effect

   D. an unexpected unfavorable effect

5. Below is a table showing backpacks and their features.

	Comfortable Straps	Weather-proof	Stylish	TOTAL
Messenger bag	1	0	1	2
Single-strap backpack	1	1	1	3
Double-strap backpack	1	1	0	2

   What is the name for this type of table?

   A. a trade-off

   B. a prototype

   C. a Pugh chart

   D. a risk-benefit analysis

Systems

Choose the letter of the best answer.

1. Which of the following most likely regulates a sprinkler system that is triggered when there is a fire?

   A. a person

   B. a manual control

   C. positive feedback

   D. an automatic control

2. Which of the following is not true of a system?

   A. A system is a distinct physical entity.

   B. A system has both inputs and outputs.

   C. A system has processes that take place within the system.

   D. A system is made of components that are isolated from one another.

3. Which statement most accurately describes two interconnected systems?

   A. A change in one system affects the other system.

   B. A change in one part of one system affects the same part of the other system.

   C. An improvement to one system causes a similar improvement to the other system.

   D. Positive feedback from one system causes negative feedback in the other system.

4. How does a control help a system?

   A. It regulates the system and makes it efficient.

   B. It organizes the system's components into related categories.

   C. It keeps the system from interacting with the outside environment.

   D. It transforms negative feedback into positive feedback.

5. Which of the following is the best example of an input added to a system?

   A.
   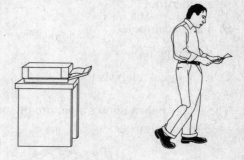

   B.

   C.

   D.

Materials and Tools

Choose the letter of the best answer.

1. What type of tool would best be used to map a section of the ocean floor?

   A. a cyber tool

   B. a physical tool

   C. a ceramic tool

   D. a chemical analysis tool

2. The image below shows a picture of something used by an engineer.

   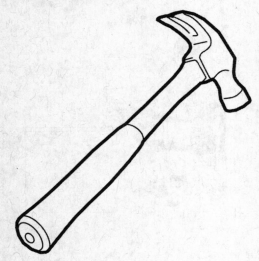

   What type of object is this?

   A. a cyber tool

   B. a physical tool

   C. a polymer material

   D. a composite material

3. Which example best represents the use of materials science in the growth of technology?

   A. the use of physical tools in large building projects

   B. the development of cyber tools for use in engineering jobs

   C. the building of an automobile prototype from metals and ceramics

   D. the creation of a stronger alloy known as steel for a variety of uses

4. Which of the following is not the correct definition of the material listed?

   A. ceramic: a material made up of two or more materials combined together

   B. polymer: a material of large molecules made by smaller molecules linking together

   C. metal: a material made out of metallic elements and held together by a metallic bond

   D. semiconductor: a material that allows electrical current, but little heat, to pass through

5. You want to build the floor of a house with marble, but you discover that marble is difficult to obtain. What type of material limitation is this?

   A. cost

   B. flexibility

   C. availability

   D. degree of hazard

Engineering and Life Science

Choose the letter of the best answer.

1. What is an example of how a product can be created using the physical structure of a living thing?

   A. spider silk from a spider

   B. antibiotics from bacteria

   C. barnacle glue from a barnacle

   D. airplane wing from a bird's wing

2. A person uses eyeglasses to see more clearly. What is the term for this kind of technological application?

   A. a medical procedure

   B. an assistive technology

   C. a medicinal technology

   D. a genetic modification

3. In the following picture, a scientist is injecting a tomato with fluid prepared in a lab.

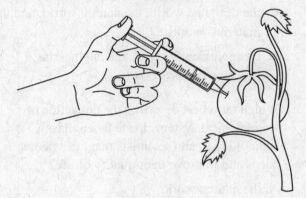

   What technological process is this picture most likely showing?

   A. product design

   B. selective breeding

   C. genetic modification

   D. medicinal formulation

4. Which of the following incorrectly states the relationship between technology and living organisms?

   A. Technology cannot change living organisms.

   B. Living organisms can be a type of technology.

   C. New technologies can be inspired by living organisms.

   D. Technology can help living organisms with their life processes.

5. Living organisms are typically incorporated into the technological process to make which of the following products?

   A. bread

   B. gasoline

   C. prosthetics

   D. airplane wings

Engineering and Our World

Choose the letter of the best answer.

1. Which of the following best explains why people develop technology?

   A. Technology is developed to maintain the natural order.

   B. Technology is developed to meet people's wants and needs.

   C. Technology is developed to completely replace older processes.

   D. Technology is developed to decrease efficiency of processes.

2. Car exhaust contributes to smog and acid rain, as illustrated in this picture.

   In this example, what kind of effect is smog?

   A. a trade-off

   B. a social norm

   C. a positive effect

   D. a negative effect

3. In the past, many people stored computer data on floppy disks. Eventually, people began to use compact discs with greater storage capacity. Which of the following best describes this situation?

   A. technology leading to a less useful means of storage

   B. technology being used to create a new need or want

   C. technology being used to develop the designed world

   D. technology leading to the development of new technology

4. Decisions about technology most often include examining the trade-offs between which areas?

   A. environment, society, and economics

   B. interdependence, society, and engineering

   C. the designed world, the natural world, and the materials world

   D. technological systems and engineering products and processes

5. Which term best describes the collection of technological systems made by engineers, technologists, and scientists that meet people's needs and improve their quality of life?

   A. the natural world

   B. the designed world

   C. the life science world

   D. the materials science world

The Engineering Design Process

Alternative Assessment

Climb the Ladder: *Engineering and Technology*

1. Work on your own, with a partner, or with a small group.

2. Choose one item from each rung of the ladder. Check your choices.

3. Have your teacher approve your plan.

4. Submit or present your results.

__ The End of Papers?	__ Design a Mobile
Some people argue that newspapers no longer meet individuals' needs as well as newer communications technologies do, and that newspapers will soon die out. Write a persuasive essay arguing for or against this idea.	A mobile is a sculpture with balanced parts that move. Create a mobile using the engineering design process. After you build and test your prototype, revise it until the mobile is balanced. Present your mobile to the class and describe your process.
__ Underwater Lab	__ Adaptive Devices
Your company has been hired to build an underwater laboratory where scientists can live and work. The company's engineers have drawn up a design; now it's your job to plan a prototype. Write a proposal, explaining what type of model you intend to use and why.	Adaptive devices are technologies that help people physical with disabilities perform everyday tasks. Research adaptive devices and create a poster that shows some types of devices and how they help people solve everyday problems.
__ Constraints	__ Job Description
You work for a toy company that makes building sets for children ages two to four. List at least four constraints that you need to consider when designing products for this age group.	Your company is developing paint that can last 50 years without peeling or fading. Write a job description that tells what type of skills and educational background candidates need to work on the project.

Methods of Analysis

Mix and Match: *Analyzing Technology*

Mix and match ideas to show what you've learned about how scientists and engineers evaluate technology.

1. Work on your own, with a partner, or with a small group.

2. Choose one information source from Column A, two ways to analyze the technology from Column B, and one option to communicate your analysis from Column C. Check your choices.

3. Have your teacher approve your plan.

4. Submit or present your results.

A. Choose One Information Source	B. Choose Two Things to Analyze	C. Choose One Way to Communicate Analysis
___ observations of a technology	___ the expected, unexpected, favorable, and unfavorable effects of the technology	___ poster with both text and illustrations
___ print or Internet technological specifications of a product	___ trade-offs associated with the manufacture or use of the technology	___ pamphlet designed to share information with others
___ print or Internet consumer information about a technology	___ risk-benefit analysis of the use of the technology	___ newspaper-style article about the technology, with illustrations
___ an interview with an individual who is knowledgable about a type of technology	___ life cycle analysis of the technology from production through disposal	___ multimedia presentation
_____	___ Pugh chart comparing the technology to other similar technologies	_____

Systems

Alternative Assessment

Mix and Match: *System Efficiency*
Mix and match ideas to show what you've learned about systems, their components, and interactions between spheres.

1. Work on your own, with a partner, or with a small group.

2. Choose one information source from Column A, three topics from Column B, and one option from Column C. Check your choices.

3. Have your teacher approve your plan.

4. Submit or present your results.

A. Choose One Information Source	B. Analyze These Three Things	C. Choose One Way to Communicate Analysis
___ observations of a home security system	___ The system's input, output, and method of control	___ diagram or illustration
___ observations of a school heating and cooling system	___ The system's feedback methods and interactions with other systems	___ colors or symbols marked on a visual, with a key
___ observations of a car or truck	___ The system's effectiveness and ways to make the system work better	___ model, such as drawings or descriptions connected by strings
___ observations of a bicycle		___ booklet, such as a field guide, travel brochure, or playbook
___ observations of a golf course sprinkler system		___ multimedia presentation
___ observations of a city transportation system		___ mathematical depiction, perhaps explaining relative numbers or component counts
___ observations of an evacuation plan		
_____		_____

Alternative Assessment

Materials and Tools

Mix and Match: *The Tools You Use*
Mix and match ideas to show what you've learned about roles in energy transfer.

1. Work on your own, with a partner, or with a small group.

2. Choose one information source from Column A, two topics from Column B, and one option from Column C. Check your choices.

3. Have your teacher approve your plan.

4. Submit or present your results.

A. Choose One Information Source	B. Choose Two Things to Analyze	C. Choose One Way to Communicate Analysis
____ experimental testing of the properties of two or more materials	____ Explain how testing is important for tools and materials.	____ diagram or illustration
____ Internet resource about materials science	____ Compare properties of two or more materials.	____ timeline, showing dates and images
____ a library book about materials or materials science	____ Relate properties of materials with their uses.	____ demonstration, with an explanation
____ case study of a tool or technology, its modifications, and the materials it interacts with	____ Describe how new tools improve materials.	____ booklet, such as a materials brochure, resource guide, or tools manual.
	____ Describe how new materials improve tools.	____ game
	____ Explain how new tools and materials impact people and society.	____ story, song, or poem, with supporting details
_____	____ Identify a problem and how materials science provides a solution.	____ skit, chant, or dance, with supporting details
		____ multimedia presentation
		____ mathematical depiction, perhaps comparing data on properties of different materials
		_____

Engineering and Life Science

Alternative Assessment

Tic-Tac-Toe: *Technology Live!*

Pretend you work for a company that uses life sciences to develop new technologies.

1. Work on your own, with a partner, or with a small group.

2. Choose three ongoing projects happening within the company. Check the boxes you plan to complete. They must form a straight line in any direction.

3. Have your teacher approve your plan.

4. Do each activity, and turn in your results.

__ Biomimicry	__ Company Brochure	__ Executive Chef
Sketch a new technology inspired by the movements of a flying squirrel. Identify two features of flying squirrels that influenced your design and explain the purpose of your invention. Present your plan to the president of the company.	Make an informational pamphlet explaining the different aspects of life science and engineering in which your company is involved. Include sections on application of biotechnology, genetic technology, medical technology, and biomimicry.	Imagine you work in the cafeteria. Create a new recipe using at least two foods that are made with the help of organisms and at least one food that resulted from selective breeding. Make a sign describing how biotechnology was used to make the dish.
__ Then to Now	__ Trading Cards	__ Crazier Glue
Create a picture timeline describing any advancement in biotechnology. Your timeline should include three changes in a medical device or procedure, or in an organism itself. It might even include an example of biomimicry that has been improved upon over time.	Make a set of five trading cards showing five different organisms that are examples of biotechnology. Include organisms that have been changed by selective breeding and genetic engineering. Add a picture and description on how the organism is a useful tool.	You have invented a new glue based on the natural material barnacles use to attach themselves to ships. Develop the packaging for this product. It should have a name, catchy graphics, and details about the glue's design, use, and relationship to barnacles.
__ Amazing Bacteria	__ Cat's Meow	__ Film Crew
Make a public service announcement (PSA) for print or television that educates the public about the benefits of bacteria. Describe how bacteria are useful in everyday life and how they can be genetically engineered.	Write a press release about a cat your company has genetically engineered to glow when exposed to ultraviolet light. Explain the basic steps of genetic engineering that you followed.	Your company has been featured in a documentary on life-science-based engineering. Role play a scene that provides four real-life examples of how engineering and technology are related to life science.

Engineering and Our World

Points of View: *Engineering, Technology, and Society*

Your class will work together to show what you've learned about the relationship between engineering, technology, and society. You will examine this relationship from several different viewpoints.

1. Work in groups as assigned by your teacher. Each group will be assigned to one or two viewpoints.

2. Complete your assignment, and present your perspective to the class.

Examples Identify one specific example of a technology that has affected society. Then, list at least ten specific effects that this technology has had on society. State your opinion on whether each of these effects is positive or negative.

Illustrations Make a collage that shows images associated with engineering, technology, and society. For example, a picture of a traffic jam on a highway shows how a technology created through engineering (the automobile) can impact people's lives. For each image you include, write a caption summarizing how the image shows the relationship between engineering, technology, and society.

Analysis Consider the following question: Do changes in technology that occur in response to consumers' wants always lead to improved technology? In other words, are the changes in technology sought after by consumers always for the best in terms of the environment and other impacts on society? Consider several specific examples of change in technology to develop a response to this question. Then, share your response and the examples in a paragraph.

Observations Identify one aspect of your life in which you can clearly observe the effects of a specific technology. Then, each member of the group should take notes over a one-week period describing the effects of this technology on his or her life. Develop a presentation of the information the group has gathered.

Models Think about the interrelationship between technology and society; then, develop a diagram that shows the ways in which they affect each other.

Selecting Materials

Purpose Students will test multiple adhesives to determine which adhesive is most appropriate to solve a problem.

Time Period 30 minutes on each of two days

Preparation Students will use 30 minutes on the first day to apply various adhesives and another 30 minutes on a second day to review and analyze the results. Provide students with several different types of adhesives, such as craft glue, rubber cement, wood glue, epoxy, and other types of adhesives. When students are making observations, encourage them to consider properties other than only how well the adhesive keeps the materials together.

Be sure to select adhesives that are safe for students to use. Provide gloves so that students do not touch the adhesives with their hands.

Safety Tips Do not eat or inhale adhesives. Wear gloves when using adhesives.

Teaching Strategies This activity works best when students work in small groups.

Scoring Rubric

Possible points	Performance indicators
0–20	Extent of participation in group activity
0–40	Appropriate use of materials and equipment
0–40	Analysis of materials

Selecting Materials

Objective

When engineers design a product, they must choose the materials that are best suited for the task. In this activity, you will compare several adhesives and then choose the adhesive that is best for different applications.

Know the Score!

As you work through this activity, keep in mind that you will be earning a grade for the following:

- how much you participate with your group (20%)
- how well you work with materials and equipment (40%)
- how you analyze the materials (40%)

Materials and Equipment

- adhesives, 3 types
- paper, tissue, small pieces (12)
- paper (3)

- polystyrene foam, small pieces (12)
- sponge, small pieces (12)
- wood, craft shapes or blocks (12)

Safety Information ◆

Do not inhale or eat adhesives. Wear gloves when using adhesives.

Procedure

1. Select three adhesives.

2. Label one sheet of paper with the name of one of the adhesives.

3. Use the adhesive to glue a piece of each type of material to another piece of the same material. For example, glue a piece of sponge to another piece of sponge. Make observations on the piece of paper.

4. Use the same adhesive to glue each type of material to each of the other types of material. For example, glue a piece of sponge to a piece of polystyrene. Make observations on the piece of paper.

5. Repeat Steps 2 to 4 for each of the other adhesives.

6. Leave the samples in a safe place for one day.

7. After a day, observe the samples again. Gently pull the samples apart.

Analysis

8. Describe some differences between the adhesives you observed.

_____

_____

_____

9. Did any of the adhesives seem to work better than others? Explain your answer.

_____

_____

_____

10. Other than how well the adhesives held the materials together, what are other advantages and disadvantages of each adhesive?

_____

_____

_____

11. What adhesive would you use to repair a wooden chair leg? Why?

_____

_____

Unit 3: Engineering, Technology and Society

Vocabulary
Fill in each blank with the term that best completes the following sentences.

1. Applying science and mathematics to solve real-world problems is called _____ .

    A. trade-off

    B. risk-benefit analysis

    C. engineering

    D. materials science

2. Testing and evaluating a(n) _____ is an important step in the design process.

    A. prototype   C. output

    B. system   D. control

3. Engineers perform a(n) _____ to compare the possible negative effects of making a decision involving technology with the possible positive effects.

    A. life cycle analysis   C. prototype

    B. input   D. risk-benefit analysis

4. To determine how a technology might affect the environment from the time it is made, sold, and used to the time it must be disposed of, engineers do a(n) _____ .

    A. Pugh chart   C. control

    B. life cycle analysis   D. trade-off

5. The information, material, energy, or any components that an engineer adds to a system are called

    _____ .

    A. inputs

    B. feedback

    C. systems theory

    D. outputs

Key Concepts
Read each question below, and circle the best answer.

6. Which statement best describes technology?

    A. the tools, machines, materials, and processes that are used for practical purposes

    B. the application of science and mathematics to solve problems that meet the needs of society and improve the quality of life

    C. the study of the natural world

    D. the exploration of the nature of science

7. Krisha and many of her friends bought a new kind of cell phone that they used to make calls, text, and send pictures. Soon, they had trouble getting their phones to connect and stay connected. What was the most likely cause of the problem?

A. Krisha and her friends did not know how to operate the cell phones.

B. The phones were old and worn out.

C. The popularity of the new phones had the unintended effect of overloading the cell phone system.

D. The new phones were not designed to be used as cell phones.

8. Raoul is studying areas of the United States to find the best location for high-rise senior citizen housing.

Major Earthquakes in Northern California						
Year	1906	1911	1979	1980	1984	1989
Magnitude	7.8	6.5	5.7	5.8	6.2	6.9

To help with his decision on the best location, how could Raoul use this table listing the major earthquakes that have occurred in northern California?

A. to develop a list of building materials

B. to perform a life cycle analysis

C. to create a model

D. to perform a risk-benefit analysis

9. Which of the following is not a tool used in engineering and technology?

A. computer design program

C. suspension bridge

B. electron microscope

D. power drill

10. Technology used in developing automobiles had some unintended effects.

What unintended effect does the illustration show?

A. Automobile technology led to traffic jams in urban areas.

B. Technology used in developing internal combustion engines led to exhaust gases that pollute the environment.

C. Automobile use led to highway accidents.

D. Factories for building automobiles led to jobs and increased economic benefits.

11. Look at the image of a dam.

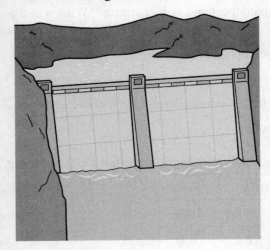

What class of materials did engineers choose to build the poured concrete walls of this dam?

A. metals

C. polymers

B. ceramics

D. semiconductors

12. Rosa made this chart when she was studying the properties of various materials.

Material	Time for temperature to increase by 10 degrees (hours)
plastic foam	5.10
ceramic	3.20

In what engineering design project would Rosa find this information useful?

A. deciding on material for improved building insulation

B. deciding on new composite materials for athletic shoes

C. deciding on stronger street-paving materials

D. deciding on material for a lightweight, but strong, automobile body

13. Look at the diagram of DNA.

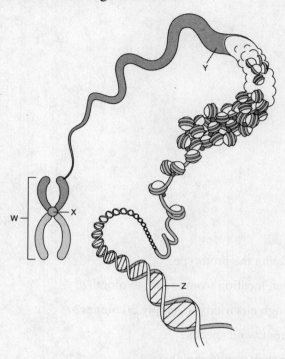

The spot labeled Z shows a place where a genetic engineer could use a "chemical scissors" to cut the DNA. Why might a genetic engineer want to cut DNA?

A. to create a new organism through selective breeding

B. to study and learn more about what makes up DNA

C. to insert a gene from a bacterium that will make a protein for use as a drug

D. to create a large model of DNA

14. Iona made a list of four advances in technology that were inspired by living things. She listed one item in error. Which item should not be on Iona's list?

A. cardboard boxes for shipping goods

B. wings on airplanes

C. a drug for treating diabetes by controlling blood sugar

D. flippers scuba divers wear on their feet to help them swim

15. The social need to have living space, offices, and stores located in a downtown area led to technologies for constructing very tall buildings. Which of the following needs most likely came about because of the new building technology?

A. the need for technology to develop better lighting

B. the need for better street paving materials

C. the need for new communications technology

D. the need for technology to develop elevators

16. Engineers built and used a prototype, based on the sketch below, to answer questions about the best design for a windmill to generate electricity.

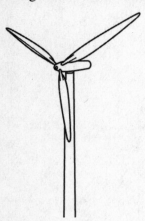

Which of these questions could not be answered by studying the prototype?

A. What would the wind speed and direction be at a given location from month to month?

B. What rotation speed of the blades could produce enough electricity to supply 20 homes?

C. How rapidly would the windmill blades turn at different wind speeds?

D. Would the blades produce high levels of sound when they turned rapidly?

Critical Thinking
Answer the following questions in the space provided.

17. A pot of boiling water on a stove is a system. What action could you take to make the pot of water an open system? What action would make it a closed system? In terms of the pot of boiling water, what is happening in the closed system that does not happen in the open system?

_____

_____

_____

18. The development of refrigeration and frozen food technology has benefitted society in different ways. Identify two ways in which refrigeration has helped people. Name two products that developed because of frozen food technology.

_____

_____

_____

19. Kaseem included a thermostat in a diagram of his home's heating system. A thermostat is a part of the feedback system within the heating system. What type of system component is a thermostat? What does the thermostat use as feedback, and how does this feedback system cause the heating system to turn on?

_____

_____

_____

_____

Connect ESSENTIAL QUESTIONS

Lessons 1, 2, 4, and 6

Answer the following question in the space provided.

20. Charlia is creating a design for an airplane that can carry 1,500 to 3,000 people. Why would there be a need for such an airplane? What properties should the material have for the wings and body? What types of trade-off could there be in using a very expensive, new material? How could Charlia go about improving an existing material?

_____

_____

_____

_____

Name _____ Date _____

Engineering, Technology and Society

Key Concepts
Choose the letter of the best answer.

1. The following table lists characteristics of four different materials.

	Make-up	Properties
Material A	metallic elements	dense, strong, flexible, able to transfer energy and electricity well
Material B	inorganic compounds	brittle, strong, does not transfer energy and electricity well
Material C	large molecules formed from smaller molecules linking together	not dense, does not transfer energy and electricity well
Material D	combination of materials	depends on the meterials that make it up

What type of material is Material D?

A. a metal

B. a ceramic

C. a polymer

D. a composite

2. What is the best example of the designed world?

A. a city

B. a park

C. a rural town

D. a countryside

3. Which of the following is the best example of a technology changing over time to become more efficient?

A. automobiles being equipped with airbags to protect people in accidents

B. cell phones being redesigned to feature different colors, shapes, and ring tones

C. personal computers becoming smaller while being able to perform more operations

D. solar cells becoming more widespread to generate electricity without burning fossil fuels

4. The image on the left shows a bullet train, and the image on the right shows the beak of a bird called a kingfisher.

Which of the following conclusions is most justified by these images?

A. The kingfisher is able to fly nearly as fast as the bullet train can move.

B. The materials used to make bullet trains come from environments populated by kingfishers.

C. The kingfisher's beak structure inspired engineers to construct the shape of the bullet train's nose.

D. The design of the bullet train inspired scientists to modify the genetic structure of the kingfisher.

5. During which step of the engineering design process would a prototype most likely be created?

A. conducting research

B. testing and evaluating

C. identifying a problem

D. communicating the results

6. Which of the following is the best example of the interdependence of society and technology?

A. The invention of the radio helped to pave the way for the invention of the television.

B. The invention of the telescope allowed people to discover new planets and stars far from Earth.

C. The invention of the automobile resulted in people living farther from where they work and shop.

D. The invention of sign language gave people who could not hear or speak another way to communicate.

7. Which of the following is the best example of technology helping a person complete life processes?

   A. pads protect a person playing sports

   B. a computer allows a person to access the Internet

   C. a wheelchair moves a person who has lost the use of his legs

   D. a binder makes it easier for a person to organize documents needed for class

8. The following Pugh Chart lists characteristics of various types of transportation over a distance of 200 miles.

	Cost	Comfort	Speed	Ease of Use	TOTAL
Walking	3	0	0	0	3
Car	2	1	2	3	8
Train	1	2	1	1	5
Airplane	0	3	3	2	8

   According to this chart, what is the least desirable way to travel a distance of 200 miles?

   A. by car

   B. by train

   C. by airplane

   D. by walking

9. Turning up the heat during cold weather increases one's comfort, but the technology requires electricity. Most electricity is generated by burning fossil fuels, which pollutes the air. To reduce electricity use, energy companies suggest that people turn down the heat when they're not home and wear heavier clothes when they are home. What best describes this practice?

   A. a trade-off in which a certain benefit is used to gain another benefit

   B. a trade-off in which a certain benefit is lost to minimize a harmful effect

   C. a trade-off in which a small negative effect is allowed to gain a large benefit

   D. a trade-off in which a small negative effect leads to a more significant negative effect

10. A computer is a type of system, with many inputs and outputs. Which of the following is most directly responsible for inputs?

    A. printer

    B. speaker

    C. keyboard

    D. headphones

11. Which of the following is the best example of interconnected technological systems?

   A. A person works up a sweat after going for a run, then cools off by taking a shower.

   B. A person rides a bicycle over a nail in the road, which causes the bicycle's tire to burst.

   C. A person increases the heat setting on a thermostat, which sends a signal that turns on the furnace.

   D. A person places several different fruits into a blender, then turns on the blender to make a fruit smoothie.

12. To make the following working model of a solar-powered car, the design team first determined which materials have previously been used to create similar models.

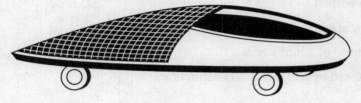

   What engineering skill would have been most necessary to answer this question?

   A. modeling skills

   B. research skills

   C. mathematics skills

   D. brainstorming skills

13. For which of the following applications is a meterstick most appropriate?

   A. determining the length that a bridge must be to span a river

   B. determining the maximum weight that an elevator can safely carry

   C. determining the speed that an airplane must travel before it can take off

   D. determining the proportions that a shelf must have to fit on top of a desk

14. Many homes have heating and cooling systems installed. Which term best describes the beginning temperature of the home, before the heating or cooling system turns on?

A. an input

B. a control

C. an output

D. a feedback

15. Which of the following is an example of an organism being used for a technological application?

A. Algae produce oils that people turn into biofuel.

B. Cows produce milk that people drink for nutrition.

C. The shape of a train is inspired by the shape of a bird's beak.

D. The habitat of a species of bear is threatened by a highway's construction.

Critical Thinking

Answer the following questions in the space provided.

16. Modified materials are often used to make new or improved technologies. What is an example of a material that has been modified to be used in a new or improved technology?

_____

_____

Did this technology add value to society? Why or why not?

_____

_____

Extended Response
Answer the following questions in the space provided.

17. You are trying to determine what technology to use for an experiment you are conducting at school. You want something that is easy to use, small, and fast. You decide that you need a Pugh chart to figure out the best option. Here is the information you will need to plug into your Pugh chart.

Technology A = ease of use (2), size (0), speed (1)

Technology B = ease of use (1), size (1), speed (0)

Technology C = ease of use (0), size (0), speed (1)

Technology D = ease of use (1), size (1), speed (2)

In the table provided below, create a Pugh chart using the information provided above.

According to the Pugh Chart, what technology should you use? Explain your answer.

_____

_____

_____

What other factors could be included in this Pugh chart that would help you make a more informed decision?

_____

_____

_____

Engineering, Technology and Society

Key Concepts
Choose the letter of the best answer.

1. The following table lists characteristics of four different materials.

	Make-up	Properties
Material A	metallic elements	dense, strong, flexible, high electrical conductivity
Material B	inorganic compounds	brittle, strong, low electrical conductivity
Material C	large molecules formed from smaller molecules linking together	low density, low electrical conductivity
Material D	combination of materials	low density, good insulator, low conductivity

What material would you most likely use if you were an electrician and wanted to connect a light to the source of electricity in a home?

A. Material A

B. Material B

C. Material C

D. Material D

2. What is the best example of the designed world?

A. a desert

B. a city

C. a mountain

D. a rainforest

3. Which of the following is the best example of a technology changing over time in response to a social problem?

A. cell phones being redesigned to feature different colors, shapes, and ring tones

B. personal computers becoming smaller while being able to perform more operations

C. solar cells becoming more widespread to generate electricity without burning fossil fuels

D. video editing software being created to take advantage of increasing numbers of people who own digital cameras

4. The image on the left shows a bullet train, and the image on the right shows the beak of a bird called a kingfisher.

Which of the following would make the best caption for these images?

A. Technology can help organisms carry out their life processes.

B. Organisms are often used as part of technological processes.

C. Technology is sometimes used to modify the DNA of an organism.

D. A living organism's structure can inspire the design of a product.

5. When designing technology, designers must consider factors that limit the design. What are these factors called?

A. trade-offs

B. constraints

C. prototypes

D. methodical thinking

6. Which of the following is the best example of the interdependence between technology and the environment?

A. The invention of the telephone allowed people to communicate over very long distances.

B. The invention of the automobile resulted in increased air pollution from vehicle emissions.

C. The invention of the steam engine helped to pave the way for the invention of the internal combustion engine.

D. The invention of photographs and motion pictures gave people the opportunity to experience places they could not actually visit.

7. Which of the following is the best example of an adaptive technology?

   A. a dialysis machine cleans the blood of a person suffering from kidney failure

   B. a computer provides a person with a place to store her music and documents

   C. a pick-up truck helps a person to transport heavy materials across long distances

   D. a microscope allows a person to study organisms that would otherwise be too tiny to see

8. The following Pugh Chart lists characteristics of various types of transportation over a distance of 200 miles.

	Cost	Comfort	Speed	Ease of Use	TOTAL
Walking	3	0	0	0	3
Car	2	3	1	3	9
Train	1	2	2	2	7
Airplane	0	1	3	2	6

   According to this chart, what is the best way to travel a distance of 200 miles?

   A. by car

   B. by train

   C. by airplane

   D. by walking

9. Many people who have a disease called multiple sclerosis use drugs called interferons to help keep the disease at bay. Even though interferons give most people who take them flu-like symptoms, people still take them. What best describes this scenario?

   A. a trade-off in which a certain benefit is lost to gain another benefit

   B. a trade-off in which a certain benefit is used to gain another benefit

   C. a trade-off in which a small negative effect is allowed to gain a large benefit

   D. a trade-off in which a small negative effect leads to a more significant negative effect

10. A computer is a type of system, with many inputs and outputs. Which of the following is most directly responsible for outputs?

    A. mouse

    B. printer

    C. electricity

    D. keyboard

11. Which of the following is the best example of interconnected technological systems?

    A. A person swings a baseball bat to hit a baseball, then runs around the bases.

    B. A person rides a bicycle down a steep hill, which causes the bicycle to increase speed.

    C. A person selects the "Print" function on a computer, which causes a printer to print the person's document.

    D. A person mixes several different ingredients to make a cake batter, then places the batter in the oven to bake.

12. The image shows a design for a solar powered car.

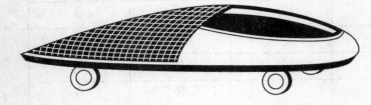

What is the most likely reason the designers of this car would have needed to use research skills?

    A. The designers needed to calculate the speed at which the car is moving.

    B. The designers needed to create a three-dimensional computer model of the car.

    C. The designers needed to imagine new ways of implementing solar energy technology into cars.

    D. The designers needed to determine which materials have previously been used to create similar cars

13. For which of the following applications are physical tools most appropriate?

    A. modeling the effects of a weather system that may move into an area

    B. modeling the speed at which a glacier moved during the most recent Ice Age

    C. modeling the differences between a human skeleton and a chimpanzee skeleton

    D. modeling the rates at which different volcanoes in the same island chain might erupt

14. Many homes have heating and cooling systems installed. What would the thermostat be termed?

   A. an input

   B. a control

   C. an output

   D. feedback

15. Yeast is a living organism that bakers often use to make dough rise. What is yeast an example of?

   A. an organism being changed by technology

   B. an organism being used to create new technology

   C. an organism being used to help with life processes

   D. an organism being used for a technological application

Critical Thinking
Answer the following questions in the space provided.

16. Describe one way that a team tasked with designing a bridge might use modified materials.

_____

_____

Explain how using materials in this way would benefit the team.

_____

_____

Extended Response
Answer the following questions in the space provided.

17. You are trying to determine what technology to use for an experiment you are conducting at school. You want something that is easy to use, small in size, and fast in speed. You decide that you need a Pugh chart to figure out the best option. Here is the information you will need to plug into your Pugh chart.

Technology A = ease of use (1), size (1), speed (2)

Technology B = ease of use (1), size (0), speed (1)

Technology C = ease of use (1), size (0), speed (0)

Technology D = ease of use (2), size (0), speed (1)

In the table provided below, create a Pugh chart using the information provided above.

According to the Pugh Chart, which technology is the least desirable option? Explain your answer.

_____

_____

_____

What is one other factor in your decision that a Pugh chart would not help you to analyze? Explain your answer.

_____

_____

_____

Introduction to Science and Technology

Choose the letter of the best answer.

1. During several trials, a group of scientists tests the reaction of a new medicine on a strain of bacteria. Which step is essential for proving the validity of the results?

    A. Make the process public so the results can be replicated.

    B. Change the procedure to check whether the same results take place.

    C. Have another scientist check to make sure the medicine was properly produced.

    D. Have each group member use a different medicine and see what happens when they test it on the bacteria.

2. The figure below shows three atomic models developed over time.

    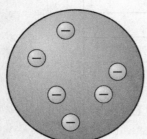 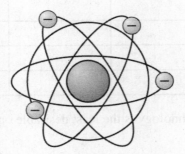 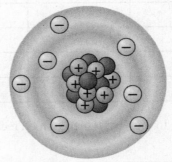

    Thomson's model of atom   Rutherford's model of atom   Current model of atom

    Which of these statements about atomic models is **most likely** correct?

    A. The atomic model has not changed over time.

    B. As scientists learned more, they modified the atomic model.

    C. Scientists are still debating which of the three theories is right.

    D. Scientists think real atoms look like a combination of the three different models.

3. In 2008, Evan B. Forde received a congressional commendation as "one of the nation's leading African-American scientists and explorers." He received the award in Jacksonville, Florida, where he works to help increase students' interest in mathematics, oceanography, and earth science. In what area has Forde's work had an impact on society?

    A. education

    B. astronomy

    C. engineering

    D. energy resources

4. Which of the following would best be represented by a conceptual model?

   A. a train

   B. a building

   C. the water cycle

   D. the formula for salt

5. A company has designed a couch using materials intended to be recycled quickly into the environment once the couch is thrown away. What type of analysis did the company most likely do on this couch?

   A. a life-cycle analysis

   B. a trade-off analysis

   C. a risk-benefit analysis

   D. a technological analysis

6. The figures below show how the model of the atom has changed over time.

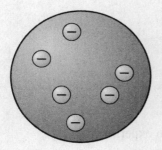 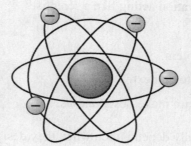 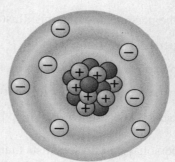

Thomson's model of atom   Rutherford's model of atom   Current model of atom

   Which of the following statements best explains why these changes happened?

   A. Scientists realized atoms were bigger then previously thought.

   B. Scientists realized atoms contain only one kind of particle at their centers.

   C. Scientists once thought positively charged particles orbit a negatively charged center, and later they reversed the picture.

   D. Scientists realized that all positive charge was located at the center of the atom and negatively charged particles, called *electrons*, moved about the center.

7. People work in many fields, such as the person shown in the following illustration.

How is the person shown in this illustration acting like a scientist?

A. The person is working hard.

B. The person is trying to solve a problem.

C. The person is thinking about what to do next.

D. The person is using a tool to help him make observations.

8. Which personal trait do scientists mainly depend upon when they design an experiment?

A. creativity

B. skepticism

C. objectivity

D. determination

9. A chemist uses a chemical formula to represent the reaction of two elements. What kind of model is the chemist using?

A. a scale model

B. a physical model

C. a conceptual model

D. a mathematical model

10. The picture shows many common household items.

What kind of material are all of these household items made of?

A. a metal

B. a ceramic

C. a polymer

D. a composite

11. Titanium is a chemical element that, when combined with other elements, can make a very strong material. Titanium is used in aircraft, missiles, spacecraft, and naval ships. What best describes titanium in this example?

A. a material that has been tested to see how well it functions

B. a material that has been changed to increase its useful properties

C. a material that is limited by the cost of extracting it from the earth

D. a material that is resistant to UV light because of it chemical properties

12. Which of the following is the best example of a closed system?

A. a car

B. an oven

C. a snowglobe

D. a food processor

13. The mayor of Fairview obtains data on his town's population. The pictograph below shows the town's population over a four-year period.

Year	Population
2005	☺ ☺ ☺ ☺
2006	☺ ☺ ☺ ☺ ☺ ☺ ☾
2007	☺ ☺ ☺ ☺ ☺ ☺
2008	☺ ☺ ☺ ☺ ☺ ☾

☺ = 1,000 people

What was the change in the town's population between 2007 and 2008?

A. It had 500 fewer people.

B. It had 1,000 fewer people.

C. It had 1,500 fewer people.

D. It had 2,000 fewer people.

14. Which description defines pseudoscience?

A. process of investigation that resembles science and follows scientific methods

B. process of investigation that resembles science, but does not follow scientific methods

C. process of investigation that does not resemble science, but follows scientific methods

D. process of investigation that does not resemble science and does not follow scientific methods

15. Look at the figure below.

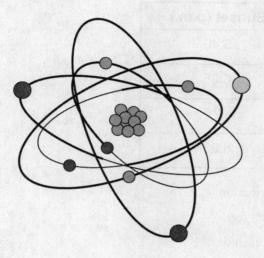

What is this an example of?

A. a model

B. a hypothesis

C. an experiment

D. an observation

16. The speed of light is 300,000,000 m/s. Which of the following represents this number in scientific notation?

A. 3.0×10^8 m/s

B. 300.0×10^6 m/s

C. 30000.0×10^4 m/s

D. 3000000.0×10^2 m/s

17. Which of the following best supports a scientific explanation?

A. hypothesis formed after initial observations

B. personal bias and the opinion of the scientist

C. imagination and originality of the hypothesis

D. experimental data obtained by using technology to get objective measurements

18. Sunrise and sunset data for Cocoa Beach, Florida, are shown in the table below.

Date	Sunrise (a.m.)	Sunset (p.m.)
January 5, 2008	7:15	5:40
March 5, 2008	6:43	6:25
May 5, 2008	6:39	?
July 5, 2008	6:31	8:23

Which conclusion can you accurately reach from this information?

A. From January to July, it gets colder in Cocoa Beach each day.

B. From January to July, there are more hours of daylight each day.

C. From January to July, the sun rises later in the morning each day.

D. From January to July, the sun sets earlier in the evening each day.

19. How would a biologist best use a computer to predict the amount of rainforest that will be destroyed over the next decade?

A. run a simulation based on trends

B. graph data from direct observations

C. create a real-time animation

D. represent indirect observations

20. How are medicines similar to adaptive technologies?

A. Both medicines and adaptive technologies are inspired by living things.

B. Both medicines and adaptive technologies help engineers develop better products.

C. Both medicines and adaptive technologies help organisms complete life processes.

D. Both medicines and adaptive technologies are primarily intended to restore a person's health.

21. Ella paints three identical pieces of metal different colors. She then makes sure they are the same temperature and places them near each other in direct sunlight for 30 minutes. She records temperature data in a table.

Color of metal	Temperature of metal (°C)
white	40
green	66
black	70

Based on the procedure and the data, which explanation tells why the temperatures are not the same?

A. Each color absorbs a different amount of heat energy.

B. A different amount of sunlight strikes each piece of metal.

C. The mass of each sample varies, which affects heat absorption.

D. The temperatures of the metal pieces vary at the beginning of the experiment.

22. A company decides to "go green" by eliminating all paperwork and completing everything within a computer database, a decision that requires a substantial up-front cost. What did the company most likely base this technological decision on?

A. economic concerns

B. cultural practices

C. societal norms

D. environmental concerns

23. When scientists obtain new information, what happens to an existing scientific theory?

A. It is revised.

B. It is reevaluated.

C. It becomes a law.

D. It remains the same.

24. The image below shows four measurements (small dots) and an actual value (large center).

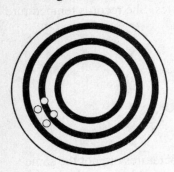

How are these measurements best described in terms of accuracy and precision?

A. The measurements are accurate and precise.

B. The measurements are accurate but not precise.

C. The measurements are precise but not accurate.

D. The measurements are neither accurate nor precise.

25. Consider what you know about the relationship between science, technology, engineering, and mathematics. Based on these relationships, which of the following is not a true statement?

A. Math is used by engineers.

B. Engineering limits science.

C. Science contributes to technology.

D. Technology is used in engineering.

26. Consider the following interaction:

1) A microphone takes in a sound.

2) The sound is amplified through a speaker and is output louder.

3) The microphone takes in the amplified sound from the speaker.

4) The sound is amplified again by the speaker and is output even louder.

Which of the following best describes the interaction between the microphone and the loudspeaker?

A. a control

B. a component

C. a positive feedback

D. a negative feedback

27. During what step of the engineering process would a scientist most likely go to the library?

A. defining the problem

B. conducting research

C. testing and evaluating

D. communicating results

28. Selective breeding has been used to create plants that are more resistant to disease. What is this an example of?

   A. an organism being used as part of a technological process

   B. an organism being changed through technological methods

   C. a new technology inspired by the natural structure of a living organism

   D. a new technology being developed directly from the structure of an organism

29. The graph shows the sales of a technological product.

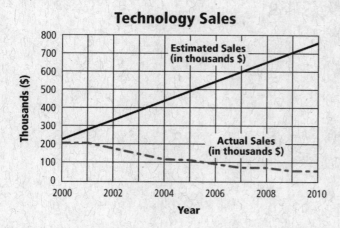

Which term would most likely describe the actual sales of this product?

   A. expected favorable

   B. expected unfavorable

   C. unexpected favorable

   D. unexpected unfavorable

30. A scientist is trying to determine the best type of material to use for an experiment. Above all, the scientist wants a material that will not corrode when exposed to different substances. What type of property is the scientist most concerned about?

   A. the physical properties

   B. the chemical properties

   C. the functional properties

   D. the compositional properties

Name _____ Date _____

End-of-Module Test
Mark one answer for each question.

1 (A) (B) (C) (D)   11 (A) (B) (C) (D)   21 (A) (B) (C) (D)

2 (A) (B) (C) (D)   12 (A) (B) (C) (D)   22 (A) (B) (C) (D)

3 (A) (B) (C) (D)   13 (A) (B) (C) (D)   23 (A) (B) (C) (D)

4 (A) (B) (C) (D)   14 (A) (B) (C) (D)   24 (A) (B) (C) (D)

5 (A) (B) (C) (D)   15 (A) (B) (C) (D)   25 (A) (B) (C) (D)

6 (A) (B) (C) (D)   16 (A) (B) (C) (D)   26 (A) (B) (C) (D)

7 (A) (B) (C) (D)   17 (A) (B) (C) (D)   27 (A) (B) (C) (D)

8 (A) (B) (C) (D)   18 (A) (B) (C) (D)   28 (A) (B) (C) (D)

9 (A) (B) (C) (D)   19 (A) (B) (C) (D)   29 (A) (B) (C) (D)

10 (A) (B) (C) (D)   20 (A) (B) (C) (D)   30 (A) (B) (C) (D)

Test Doctor

Unit 1 The Nature of Science

Unit Pretest

1. A   5. C   9. C
2. C   6. D   10. B
3. B   7. C
4. D   8. B

1. A

A is correct because an astronomer studies objects in space, such as the planets.

B is incorrect because an ecologist studies organisms and their environment.

C is incorrect because an engineer applies science to solve problems.

D is incorrect because a geologist studies Earth, including its origin and history.

2. C

A is incorrect because scientists do conduct experiments under controlled conditions.

B is incorrect because there is more than one scientifically based method for conducting investigations.

C is correct because investigations often do include multiple trials.

D is incorrect because many investigations focus on exploring unregulated surroundings.

3. B

A is incorrect because the data shows that the bacteria reproduce faster at higher temperatures.

B is correct because the bacteria reproduce fastest in the 20 °C to 30 °C range.

C is incorrect because the bacteria reproduce faster at lower temperatures.

D is incorrect because the bacteria reproduce faster at lower temperatures.

4. D

A is incorrect because science involves the study of nonliving items, as well.

B is incorrect because science involves the observational study of the entire universe.

C is incorrect because science is based on systematic study and evidence, not on feelings and thoughts.

D is correct because science is the systematic study of natural events and conditions.

5. C

A is incorrect because a scientist looking through a telescope is not necessarily being creative.

B is incorrect because a scientist looking through a telescope is not necessarily being logical.

C is correct because a scientist looking through a telescope is being observant.

D is incorrect because a scientist looking through a telescope is not necessarily being skeptical.

6. D

A is incorrect because weather prediction is part of meteorology, not environmental science.

B is incorrect because environmental sciences do not focus on technology.

C is incorrect because environmental sciences do not focus on development of new medicines.

D is correct because conservation and protection of natural resources are of interest to environmental scientists.

7. C

A is incorrect because the organisms in the new groups existed well before 150 years ago.

B is incorrect because it does not explain the basis for creating new categories.

C is correct because scientific change when scientists find new evidence or a new way to apply existing evidence.

D is incorrect because scientists do not invent new organisms.

8. B

A is incorrect because scientific laws are not based on opinion.

B is correct because a scientific theory is an explanation that ties together various observations and facts.

C is incorrect because the statement describes a scientific law.

D is incorrect because a law, not a theory, describes what always happens under certain conditions.

9. C

A is incorrect because the student is studying the effect of carbon dioxide, not the effects of watering and weather, on the plants.

B is incorrect because the student has already found plants for the investigation. Identifying other plants in other areas introduces other variables.

C is correct because a controlled experiment will allow the student to best isolate the effect of carbon dioxide.

D is incorrect because surveys of plant preferences does not add data or insight into a study of the effects of carbon dioxide on plant growth.

10. B

A is incorrect because this is a reasonable question that can be answered through scientific investigation.

B is correct because there is no evidence supporting the idea that aliens built the pyramids.

C is incorrect because the processes of science cannot be used to determine whether a particular day will be suitable for making money.

D is incorrect because scientists can explain what happened to

ancient civilizations based on archaeological findings.

Lesson 1 Quiz

1. B   4. A
2. D   5. D
3. B

1. B

A is incorrect because the meaning of numbers beyond the mathematical sense cannot be tested or verified.

B is correct because a conclusion about a natural phenomenon is being supported by empirical evidence.

C is incorrect because finding water base on feeling an aura is an example of a pseudoscientific claim.

D is incorrect because predictions about the future based on the relative positions of heavenly bodies are examples of pseudoscientific claims.

2. D

A is incorrect because curiosity may lead to asking a question, not drawing a conclusion.

B is incorrect because objectivity is usually involved in making measurements and recording data.

C is incorrect because the student in this illustration seems happy rather than skeptical. Skepticism is a valuable trait in examining the process used and the data collected.

D is correct because the student is shown after drawing a conclusion, which is made by using the trait of logical reasoning.

3. B

A is incorrect because scientists study objects that are found in outer space, such as other planets and stars.

B is correct because a natural phenomenon cannot be investigated unless it can be closely observed, which may require special instruments such as microscopes and telescopes.

C is incorrect because scientists often investigate issues that others first raised. In many cases, the scientists uncover new information.

D is incorrect because a scientist may collaborate with others who can provide the expertise that is needed.

4. A

A is correct because pseudoscience deviates from the scientific method, but science does not.

B is incorrect because science is limited to phenomena people can observe.

C is incorrect because science systematically studies natural events and conditions.

D is incorrect because science uses a large body of empirical evidence to make explanations.

5. D

A is incorrect because peer review is the process by which scientists validate or invalidate the work of other scientists.

B is incorrect because pseudoscience is the process of investigation that deviates from the scientific method.

C is incorrect because logical reasoning is the process by which people draw valid conclusions from true statements.

D is correct because empirical evidence is the cumulative body of observations that leads to a scientific explanation of a natural phenomenon.

Lesson 2 Quiz

1. D   4. C
2. D   5. C
3. C

1. D

A is incorrect because a paper in a professional education journal has the most validity.

B is incorrect because a story in a magazine might lack some validity, but the experience of the teacher makes it credible, and it has more validity than a scientist who does one study and uses a small sample size.

C is incorrect because a journalist is citing the work of an educational researcher, which has a measure of validity.

D is correct because a small sample size and one study is

not enough to make a valid conclusion.

2. D

A is incorrect because not all lab experiments involve models.

B is incorrect because lab experiments do not involve uncontrolled conditions.

C is incorrect because lab experiments do not take place in unregulated environments.

D is correct because lab experiments must include all of these characteristics.

3. C

A is incorrect because a scientist would choose the lab to have fewer variables to study.

B is incorrect because a scientist would choose fieldwork, not a lab, to make observations under natural conditions.

C is correct because a scientist would choose the lab to have a more controlled environment.

D is incorrect because a scientist would not have a good experiment if the sample size was small, and thus would not need the lab to have a smaller sample size.

4. C

A is incorrect because the data table does not include multiple trials.

B is incorrect because the data table shows places for recording temperature at different times but does not include multiple trials.

C is correct because the data table includes multiple trials. Repetition of trials increases the sample size of the data and decreases error.

D is incorrect because the data table has places to show the beginning and ending temperatures but does not include multiple trials.

5. C

A is incorrect because the results are not valid, so forming a new hypothesis and planning a new experiment would be the correct procedure.

B is incorrect because changing data is unethical and does not produce valid results.

C is correct because the researcher needs a new hypothesis and a new plan for investigating the new hypothesis.

D is incorrect because an experimental procedure must be reproducible and cannot be altered from one trial to the next.

Lesson 3 Quiz

1. A   4. C
2. C   5. C
3. B

1. A

A is correct because empirical evidence is the cumulative body of explanations of a natural phenomenon.

B is incorrect because empirical evidence is not based on opinion.

C is incorrect because these are subjective, not objective like empirical evidence is.

D is incorrect because scientists cannot make up evidence to support a scientific investigation.

2. C

A is incorrect because the balloon does not get bigger as the temperature of the gas decreases.

B is incorrect because the balloon gets smaller as the temperature of the gas decreases, but not because gas particles are escaping.

C is correct because the faster-moving gas particles cause the balloon to get bigger as the temperature of the gas increases.

D is incorrect because the balloon does not get smaller as the temperature of the gas increases.

3. B

A is incorrect because chemists are less likely to be in the field observing organisms.

B is correct because some biologists frequently work in the field to observe organisms.

C is incorrect because physicists are less likely to be in the field observing organisms.

D is incorrect because mathematicians rarely perform fieldwork to gather information. They use computers, surveys, and calculations.

4. C

A is incorrect because a conceptual model usually shows an idea and does not generate any new empirical evidence.

B is incorrect because the scientists' results support the existing empirical evidence for the idea.

C is correct because finding new evidence may lead to the modification of a scientific idea.

D is incorrect because the experiment is flawed due to contamination or human error.

5. C

A is incorrect because both theories and law require evidence.

B is incorrect because theories and laws are based on both experimentation and observation.

C is correct because theories explain phenomena whereas laws describe them.

D is incorrect because both laws and theories can e modified as new evidence becomes available.

Lesson 4 Quiz

1. D   4. D
2. A   5. C
3. A

1. D

A is incorrect because the gold may be valuable, but it will benefit only a small group of people.

B is incorrect because the discovery of a new species may help explain some point about evolution, but it will not have an impact on society as a whole.

C is incorrect because society will not benefit from the discovery of a new star.

D is correct because this discovery may save many lives.

2. A

A is correct because a pharmacist must know about how medications (chemicals) may affect the body.

B is incorrect because a pharmacist does not need to know about objects in space, which are the focus of astronomy.

C is incorrect because a pharmacist does not have to be trained in earth sciences.

D is incorrect because meteorology is not required to become a pharmacist, who must know about prescription medications and their effects on the human body.

3. A

A is correct because the use of insulin treats diabetes, which is a medical problem.

B is incorrect because no information is given that a new technology was developed.

C is incorrect because insulin is used to treat, not prevent, a disease.

D is incorrect because the production of insulin by bacteria was an advance in medicine, not in environmental science.

4. D

A is incorrect because eating lunch is not an example of the mechanic acting like a scientist.

B is incorrect because choosing oil for a car is not the mechanic acting like a scientist.

C is incorrect because using a robotic arm to hoist a car is not an example of the mechanic acting like a scientist.

D is correct because forming a hypothesis and testing the hypothesis is the best choice for how a mechanic acts like a scientist.

5. C

A is incorrect because Fleming's contribution was in life science.

B is incorrect because Fleming's discovery of penicillin was the result of his scientific research, not engineering work.

C is correct because penicillin has been used to save many lives from bacterial infections.

D is incorrect because Fleming's discovery of penicillin did not have any direct impact on conserving natural resources.

Lesson 1 Alternative Assessment

Examples: Presentations describe life science, earth science, and physical science, and give three examples of something a scientist would study in each branch of science.

Illustrations: Cartoons or comic strips show a scientist testing an idea. Captions describe what the scien-tist is doing to test ideas.

Analysis: Interviews tell whether the scientist will decide to treat the investigation as science or pseudoscience, and why.

Observations: Lists contains 10 observations for each of two items in the classroom. Descriptions explain how the observations were made. Of the 10 observations for each item, at least one observation is in words, one is numbers with units, and another is a sketch or a diagram.

Details: Card congratulates a scientist for using certain traits when engaging in a scientific investiga-tion. Cards identify how the scientist used each trait.

Models: Flow charts describe how scientists develop and evaluate a scientific explanation, including when the data do or do not support the explanation.

Lesson 2 Alternative Assessment

Geologist: A geologist might study dinosaur fossils, volcanic layers, or good sites for oil wells in the field or in a lab analysis of field samples.

Geneticist: A geneticist might study DNA patterns in mice or making a faster growing corn plant in a structured lab experiment.

Biologist: A biologist might study DNA patterns in mice or ferret behavior in a structured lab experiment or through observation.

Naturalist: A naturalist might study ferret behavior through field observation.

Astronomer: An astronomer might study black holes through observation or modeling.

Physicist: A physicist might study black holes, a longer-lasting battery, or an energy-efficient location for a new building through observation, modeling, or a structured lab experiment.

Food chemist: A food chemist might study keeping crackers fresh for longer periods of time through observation or a structured lab experiment.

Medical researcher: A medical researcher might student DNA patterns in mice, heart disease progression through a structured lab experiment, observation, or modeling.

Botanist: A botanist might study making a faster growing corn plant through a structured lab experiment, field observation, or a lab analysis of field samples.

Volcanologist: A volcanologist might study volcanic layers near Mount St. Helens through field observation or lab analysis of field samples.

Paleontologist: A paleontologist might study dinosaur fossils through field observation or lab analysis of field samples.

Lesson 3 Alternative Assessment

Gathering Evidence: Sketch shows one way a chemist can collect empirical evidence about pollutants in a river.

What Do You Think?: Cards describe the most interesting fact learned in this lesson and how the lesson changed the way the student felt or thought about learning science.

You Ask the Questions: Quizzes contain at least five questions or activities that deal with scientific theories and laws, and include an answer key.

A Scientific Skit: Skits compare a scientific theory with the use of the word theory in a detective or mystery story.

Defending Review: Speech explains why the group of scientists should not be upset because another group of scientists has criticized the findings. Speech describes how peer review and discussion is important to establishing scientific knowledge.

An Empirical Essay: Essays define, describe, and give examples of empirical evidence. Essays also include introductions, bodies, and conclusions.

What's Your Theory?: Commercials explain what a scientific theory is and the how it is formed. Commercials also

promote a specific scientific theory.

Lesson 4 Alternative Assessment

In the News: One-paragraph summaries describe a new development or discovery in science and its importance.

Time Capsule: Timeline shows when five products were developed using science.

Person on the Street: Interviews record the responses of three people about an invention or recent scientific development.

Nature Sketch: Posters include a sketch of a natural environment and suggestions for how to protect that environment.

PSA: Three ads with artwork identify healthful behaviors that can keep people healthy.

Photo Essay: Photo essay contains at least five photos with captions of local scientific subjects.

10-50-100 Years Ago: Three-paragraph summaries identify a scientific development from the past and explain its use, importance, and whether it is still used today.

Invention Poll: Bar graph shows the views of 20 people about the most important invention or scientific development of the last 10 years.

How's It Work?: An illustrated summary tells how a scientific device works.

Write a Biography: A two-page biography describes the life and work of a scientist.

Performance-Based Assessment

See Unit 1, Lesson 2

7. Answers may vary. Sample data table:

1 MASS	Time for 5 swings (T)	Period (T/5)
Trial 1	2.3 sec	0.46
Trial 2	2.2 sec	0.44
Trial 3	2.6 sec	0.52
Average for three trials		0.47

8. Answers may vary. Sample data table similar to Step 7.

9. Answers may vary. Sample data table similar to Step 7 but with shorter times and periods.

10. Answers may vary. Sample data table similar to Step 7 but with longer times and periods.

11. Answers may vary. Sample answer: A change in the mass on the end of a pendulum does not change the period of the pendulum.

12. Answers may vary. Sample answer: Changing the length of the pendulum changes the period of the pendulum. When the string is shorter, the period is shorter. When the string is longer, the period is longer.

13. We could change the angle used to start the pendulum swinging. The best way to determine the effect of changing the variable is to perform an additional experiment using the changed angle as the only variable.

Unit Review

Vocabulary

1. **experiment** See Unit 1, Lesson
2. **theory** See Unit 1, Lesson 3
3. **data** See Unit 1, Lesson 2
4. **empirical evidence** See Unit 1, Lesson 1
5. **independent variable** See Unit 1, Lesson 2

Key Concepts

6. D	9. B	12. D
7. A	10. D	13. D
8. B	11. B	

6. D See Unit 1, Lesson 4

A is incorrect because the data does not give reasons for participation, just numbers of students who participated.

B is incorrect because the data shows a decrease, but not the reason for the decrease.

C is incorrect because the reason for the equal number of participants is not evident on the graph.

D is correct because the graph gives her data about past participation numbers.

7. A See Unit 1, Lesson 2

A is correct because even though a census count gathers data, it is not controlled or precise, or carried out in a laboratory.

B is incorrect because this type of experiment would be very controlled in a laboratory environment.

C is incorrect because the amount of light is an independent variable, or something that an observer would control or change within the lab.

D is incorrect because the experiment is taking place within a controlled lab environment.

8. B See Unit 1, Lesson 3

A is incorrect because the term "tenet" is not generally used to describe scientific laws, especially, since "tenet" can also be applied to opinions.

B is correct because a law is a widely agreed upon description of a direct relationship between two factors.

C is incorrect because a theory is an idea about why something occurs in the natural world.

D is incorrect because a hypothesis is a statement that a scientist develops in order to conduct an experiment.

9. B See Unit 1, Lesson 1

A is incorrect because astrology is not based on the scientific method.

B is correct because astrology, as a pseudoscience, is not based on the scientific method.

C is incorrect because astrology cannot be replicated by other scientists since it is not based on the scientific method and communicated among scientists in the traditional way.

D is incorrect because a pseudoscience can be developed at any time in history; the timing of the pseudoscience is unrelated to its practitioners not using the scientific method.

10. D See Unit 1, Lesson 2

A is incorrect because good scientific investigations can be replicated.

B is incorrect because control is a part of sound scientific investigations that test specific variables.

C is incorrect because large sample sizes are considered important for sound investigations.

D is correct because a small sample size might not provide an accurate picture of real relationships.

11. B See Unit 1, Lesson 2

A is incorrect because the results simply tell us that Clara's hypothesis was wrong, not necessarily why the materials performed differently.

B is correct because Clara's hypothesis was wrong, so she learned that the heavier of two materials will not keep the drink colder.

C is incorrect because Clara now knows that a heavier material will be a less effective insulator. She could instead investigate lighter materials for their insulating qualities.

D is incorrect because the results will not become more valid if Clara communicates the results to others.

12. D See Unit 1, Lesson 3

A is incorrect because a law is a description of a relationship or a fact.

B is correct because a theory is widely accepted and explains a relationship or the reason for a phenomenon.

C is incorrect because Dr. Grossman has not simply given a set of facts. Through her investigations, she has provided an explanation as to why the phenomena are as they are.

D is incorrect because many other scientists have accepted the theory, which means that it has moved far beyond the status of hypothesis.

13. D See Unit 1, Lesson 2

A is incorrect because the bands are all the same type.

B is incorrect because the same type of bands are used in this experiment, and their stretch is the change that results from the manipulation of the mass. This makes the stretch distance the dependent variable.

C is incorrect because time is not a variable at all in this experiment.

D is correct because the mass of the object stretching the bands is the variable that is being changed or manipulated.

Critical Thinking

14. See Unit 1, Lesson 2

• that a hypothesis is a testable idea or explanation that leads to scientific explanations of phenomena

• that a prediction shows a cause and effect relationship

• that the difference between a hypothesis and a prediction is that a hypothesis offers an explanation, and a prediction shows the cause and effect relationship

• an example of a hypothesis might be the statement "water mixed with manure will make the plant grow taller than the plain tap water"

• an example of a prediction might be the statement: "feeding manure to plants causes the plants to grow taller than plants that are not fed manure"

15. See Unit 1, Lesson 1

• the idea that science is limited to phenomena people can observe, with or without instruments to aid observation

• that scientific explanations are limited to those that can be tested and refuted by experimentation and observation

• that any answer to a question in science requires reevaluation when new, relevant information emerges

Connect Essential Questions

16. See Unit 1, Lesson 1 and Lesson 4

• that scientists work in many fields and thus can influence change in many different parts of society, any person who asks questions and looks for answers can be called a

scientist (some scientists work in life science, earth science, physical science)

• that scientists themselves come from many different backgrounds

• that people in all walks of life use scientific principles to do their work in society

• that scientific research has led to many life-saving discoveries, such as medicines, weather prediction, safer transport, and disease prevention, our ability to conserve and protect our resources

• that new technology has improved human lives and changed the way humans think about the world

Unit Test A
Key Concepts

1. A	5. B	9. A
2. D	6. D	10. A
3. B	7. D	11. C
4. C	8. C	12. A

1. A

A is correct because new data that results in changes to scientific ideas should be reviewed and debated.

B is incorrect because data may be accepted or rejected, but should not be changed without first being reviewed and debated.

C is incorrect because scientific laws result from empirical support, not from new data.

D is incorrect because the modification of scientific ideas is based on empirical evidence, not opinion.

2. D

A is incorrect because a scale model is not a real organism, therefore a scale model will not interact with its environment and conditions as the real organism would.

B is incorrect because a scale model is not a real organism or population of organisms, therefore a scale model will not interact with its environment and conditions as the real organism or population of organisms would.

C is incorrect because exact measurements are best made on the object itself. A scale model is based on measurements that have been made on the object.

D is correct because scale models are appropriate for studying objects that cannot be studied directly, such as those that are too large, too small, or too dangerous to be studied directly.

3. B

A is incorrect because the discovery of planets does not directly affect our health.

B is correct because vaccines prevent people from getting viral diseases.

C is incorrect because efficient fuels do not directly affect our health.

D is incorrect because uncovering the structure of the atom does not directly affect our health.

4. C

A is incorrect because a scientist needs curiosity to investigate questions about the natural world.

B is incorrect because a scientist needs imagination to inquire about the natural world and to obtain an explanation of what is happening.

C is correct because a scientist needs logic to devise an explanation for data.

D is incorrect because a scientist needs skepticism to repeat observations and evaluate designs and conclusions.

5. B

A is incorrect because increased, not reduced, pressure reduces the volume of a gas.

B is correct because the volume of a gas decreases as the pressure on the gas increases.

C is incorrect because the amount of gas in the system remains constant.

D is incorrect because the volume of gas changes when the pressure on the gas changes.

6. D

A is incorrect because scientists must never allow personal bias or opinions to affect the nature of their work.

B is incorrect because a hypothesis offers a possible explanation, but a hypothesis is used to identify test variables and issues to be explored. The hypothesis itself does not support an explanation.

C is incorrect because imagination and originality because a hypothesis is used to identify test variables and issues to be explored. The hypothesis itself does not support an explanation.

D is correct because the data obtained from objective measurements can be used to reach a valid conclusion.

7. D

A is incorrect because a theory explains why something happens. In this example, a theory of climate change is proposed.

B is incorrect because a theory explains why something happens. In this example, a theory of illness is proposed.

C is incorrect because a theory explains why something happens. In this example, a theory of plate movement is proposed.

D is correct because a scientific law describes and predicts what happens.

8. C

A is incorrect because the map shows a mountain range and rock types, which are features that geologists generally study.

B is incorrect because the map describes a mountain range and rock types, not information about living things, so it would more likely be used by a geologist rather than a biologist.

C is correct because the map shown is a geologic map, a tool used by geologists.

D is incorrect because physicists generally do not use maps of Earth's features.

9. A

A is correct because all scientific investigations require keeping accurate records.

B is incorrect because scientists may work together or separately while investigating.

C is incorrect because some investigations may use very simple and inexpensive equipment. The equipment should fit the purpose and procedure of the investigation.

D is incorrect because some investigations are done in the field or outside of the laboratory. Laboratories offer good opportunities for controlling variables, but may not be the best places for investigations if the goal is to study an organism in its natural environment or many other situations.

10. A

A is correct because the graph shows a constant speed, which supports the hypothesis.

B is incorrect because the graph shows a constant increase in speed, which does not support the hypothesis.

C is incorrect because the graph shows a constant decrease in speed, which does not support the hypothesis.

D is incorrect because the graph shows a variable increase in speed, which does not support the hypothesis.

11. C

A is incorrect because although planning ahead is a good practice in any career, it does not require scientific knowledge.

B is incorrect because this picture does not indicate that the person is making a hypothesis.

C is correct because all scientists use SI tools to take accurate measurements.

D is incorrect because using a sturdy table is not an example of using scientific knowledge.

12. A

A is correct because this statement does not have scientific backing from data or the scientific community.

B is incorrect because hundreds of scientists agreeing about a natural phenomenon is a major part of science.

C is incorrect because conclusions supported by numerous experiments are another component of science.

D is incorrect because conclusions supported by data are another component of science.

Critical Thinking
13.

- description and explanation of what must be done to change the theory (e.g., *Scientific ideas are not modified based on the results of just one experiment. Experiments must be repeated to make sure results are valid. The results of these experiments should then be discussed and debated, and scientists must agree upon a change before they will accept it*; etc.)

Extended Response
14.

- yes, plus supporting data from the graph to explain why the change is not constant (e.g., *Data from the graph shows that the change is not constant. In the first half hour, the temperature dropped about 170ºC, but the temperature only decreased by about 60ºC in the second half hour*; etc.)

- explanation of how Shakira could replicate her results (e.g., *Shakira should keep careful notes of her procedure so that she and other investigators can repeat her experiment*; etc.)

- explanation of how the cooling system could affect the experiment and how to avoid this problem (e.g., *The temperature within the laboratory is a variable that could affect the outcome of the experiment. Shakira should note the error in her experimental notes, then repeat the experiment. When she repeats the experiment, she should control the room temperature*; etc.)

Unit Test B
Key Concepts

1. A   5. D   9. B
2. B   6. A   10. A
3. C   7. A   11. D
4. D   8. A   12. B

1. A

A   is correct because scientific knowledge changes and grows as a result of new empirical evidence.

B   is incorrect because the modification of scientific ideas is based on empirical evidence, not opinion.

C   is incorrect because data may be shown to be correct or incorrect with additional investigation, but should not be changed.

D   is incorrect because designing an experiment does not lead to modifying the idea. Only new evidence would do that.

2. B

A   is incorrect because a model of an ecosystem does not show how people view climate change.

B   is correct because a survey would be able to determine people's views about climate change.

C   is incorrect because a laboratory experiment on the effects of climate change does not address the way people view climate change.

D   is incorrect because conducting fieldwork on gases does not address the way people view climate change.

3. C

A   is incorrect because the discovery of planets does not directly affect our ease of transportation.

B   is incorrect because transportation has not been eased by vaccines.

C   is correct because the development of the airplane has directly affected the ease of transportation.

D   is incorrect because uncovering the structure of the atom does not directly affect our ease of transportation.

4. D

A   is incorrect because a scientist always needs objectivity to make accurate measurements. He needs curiosity when investigating questions about the natural or physical world.

B   is incorrect because the scientist always needs objectivity to make accurate measurements. She needs creativity when designing experiments and devising explanations of data.

C   is incorrect because the scientist always needs

objectivity to make accurate measurements. He needs logic when reasoning, solving problems, and devising explanations of data.

D   is correct because the scientist always needs objectivity to take accurate measurements. Measurements and observations must not depend on the mood or personal bias of the people making them.

5. D

A   is incorrect because scientific laws do not describe why something happens. Instead, they describe what happens.

B   is incorrect because Boyle's law describes the effect of pressure, not temperature, on a gas.

C   is incorrect because Boyle's law does not explain what happens to the volume of a gas because of temperature change.

D   is correct because Boyle's law describes the effect of pressure on a constant mass of gas in a closed system that is kept at the same temperature.

6. A

A   is correct because anything that can be closely observed, with or without instruments, is a legitimate subject for a scientist to study.

B   is incorrect because a scientist can study something that can be detected with any of the five senses, including sight and smell.

C   is incorrect because a scientist can use instruments, such as microscopes and telescopes, to study the natural world.

D   is incorrect because a scientist may not be able to explain his or her observations.

7. A

A   is correct because a law states what happens.

B   is incorrect because a theory states why something happens.

C   is incorrect because a hypothesis is a testable idea as to what is happening, but it has not had enough testing to make it a law or a theory.

D   is incorrect because an observation describes a singular event; it does not make an all-encompassing statement.

8. A

A   is correct because during field investigations, geologists gather samples and make observations to identify the types of rock in an area.

B   is incorrect because physical modeling may provide information about geological formations, but it is not a very practical way to develop a map of an area.

C   is incorrect because laboratory experiments may be performed on rock samples taken from the area examined, but the rock samples must be collected during fieldwork.

D   is incorrect because surveys of people who live in the area would not provide reliable evidence about geologic features.

9. B

A   is incorrect because a good scientific investigation would have a large sample size.

B   is correct because if the results of a scientific investigation cannot be replicated, the investigation may be flawed.

C   is incorrect because keeping accurate records is part of a good scientific investigation.

D   is incorrect because repeating trials is part of a good scientific investigation.

10. A

A   is correct because the graph shows a constant speed, which does not support the hypothesis.

B   is incorrect because the graph shows a constant increase in speed, which supports the hypothesis.

C   is incorrect because the graph shows a constant decrease in speed, which supports the hypothesis.

D   is incorrect because the graph shows a variable increase in speed, which supports the hypothesis.

11. D

A   is incorrect because although planning ahead is a good practice in any career, it does not require scientific knowledge.

B   is incorrect because everyone must be sure to use the proper tools, a process that does not require any scientific knowledge.

C   is incorrect because taking one's time may avoid mistakes, but it does not require scientific knowledge.

D   is correct because all scientists use the metric system when making measurements.

12. B

A   is incorrect because hundreds of scientists agreeing about a natural phenomenon is a major part of science.

B   is correct because this belief is not supported by scientific evidence.

C   is incorrect because conclusions supported by many are another component of science.

D   is incorrect because conclusions supported by numerous experiments are another component of science.

Critical Thinking
13.

• prediction of how scientists will react and explanation of this answer (e.g., *Scientific ideas are not modified based on the results of just one experiment. Scientific ideas should be modified only after debate and discussion. The scientists will probably not accept the revision, because it is based on only one experiment and has not been repeated or debated with other scientists*; etc.)

Extended Response

14.

- thermometer

- yes, plus supporting data from the graph to explain why the change is not constant (e.g., *in the first half hour, the temperature dropped about 170°C, but the temperature only decreased by about 60°C in the second half hour*; etc.)

- description of how Shakira could replicate her results (e.g., *Shakira could repeat her experiment; run multiple trials; ask others to attempt to repeat the experiment*; etc.)

- explanation of how the cooling system could affect the experiment and how to avoid this problem (e.g., *The temperature within the laboratory is a variable that could affect the outcome of the experiment. Shakira should note the error in her experimental notes, then repeat the experiment. When she repeats the experiment, she should control the room temperature*; etc.)

Unit 2 Measurement and Data

Unit Pretest

1. C	5. B	9. B
2. C	6. A	10. C
3. D	7. D	
4. C	8. A	

1. C

A is incorrect because this is an example of a molecule consisting of 3 atoms.

B is incorrect because this is not an example of a neutron.

C is correct because this is an example of a molecule of water.

D is incorrect because this is not a DNA strand.

2. C

A is incorrect because scientific notation is the short way of representing very large or very small numbers. Metric units are based on the number 10.

B is incorrect because scientific notation is the short way of representing very large or very small numbers. A measurement is a numerical description and includes a unit.

C is correct because scientific notation is the short way of representing very large or very small numbers.

D is incorrect because scientific notation is the short way of representing very large or very small numbers.

3. D

A is incorrect because a scale model would not show growth.

B is incorrect because a physical model would not be the best tool to contrast two different growth rates.

C is incorrect because a conceptual model would not be the best tool to contrast two different growth rates.

D is correct because the problem concerns mathematical concepts, or growth rates, so a mathematical model would be the best model to use.

4. C

A is incorrect because a model represents something; it is not a method for predicting the future.

B is incorrect because a prototype cannot predict the future of an event.

C is correct because a simulation is an imitation of a function, process, or process (in this case, rising levels of atmospheric CO_2). A simulation can also be used to predict future events.

D is incorrect because probeware allows scientists to collect, interpret, and analyze data, not necessarily predict a future outcome of a current event.

5. B

A is incorrect because in 2007, the average salary was $54,000, and in 2008, the average salary was $51,000. This is a difference of $3,000, not $2,600.

B is correct because in 2007, the average salary was $54,000, and in 2008, the average salary was $51,000. This is a difference of $3,000.

C is incorrect because in 2007, the average salary was $54,000, and in 2008, the average salary was $51,000. This is a difference of $3,000, not $3,800.

D is incorrect because in 2007, the average salary was $54,000, and in 2008, the average salary was $51,000. This is a difference of $3,000, not $4,400.

6. A

A is correct because a hot plate and a test tube would be the best choices for heating a liquid.

B is incorrect because a stopwatch measures time.

C is incorrect because a thermometer measures temperature, it does not heat.

D is incorrect because although the Bunsen burner can heat a liquid, a triple beam balance is used to measure mass.

7. D

A is incorrect because the physician was the investigator.

B is incorrect because the exercises were the independent variable in this experiment.

C is incorrect because the student volunteers were the subjects of this experiment.

D is correct because the pulse rates depended on the exercises that the students performed.

8. A

A is correct because if using SI, length is measured in meters, not feet.

B is incorrect because time is measured in seconds.

C is incorrect because mass is measured in kilograms.

D is incorrect because temperature is measured in Kelvin.

9. B

A is incorrect because a simulation is not a model.

B is correct because a physical model is an object and often looks and acts like the object it represents.

C is incorrect because a structure is a physical object, not a conceptual one.

D is incorrect because a structure is a physical object, not a mathematical one.

10. C

A is incorrect because a scale model is a type of physical model that represents a real-life object.

B is incorrect because a physical model is a physical object.

C is correct because this is a diagram of the rock cycle, a conceptual model.

D is incorrect because a mathematical model is usually a formula or an equation.

Lesson 1 Quiz

1. B   4. D
2. A   5. B
3. C

1. B

A is incorrect because the independent and dependent variables may or may not be numbers.

B is correct because the independent variable is what the investigator controls, and the dependent variable changes as a result of this manipulation.

C is incorrect because the independent variable is what you control, and the dependent variable is what happens as a result of this.

D is incorrect because the independent variable is typically found in the first column of a table, and the dependent variable is typically found in the second column.

2. A

A is correct because a model is not able to reproduce everything about the phenomenon it represents.

B is incorrect because a model can be used to study things that are too dangerous to study in person, such as an erupting volcano.

C is incorrect because a model can be use to reproduce something that is too far away to see in person, such as the solar system.

D is incorrect because a model can be used to show things that are too large or small to see without assistive technology, such as a molecule.

3. C

A is incorrect because experiments are investigational processes with various steps that often require the manipulation of materials and equipment.

B is incorrect because hypotheses are testable explanations of observed phenomena.

C is correct because models are visual or mathematical representations that can be used in many different ways.

D is incorrect because observations are data that scientists collect using their senses and/or tools.

4. D

A is incorrect because the title of a line graph indicates what the graph represents.

B is incorrect because the legend of a line graph indicates what each type of line represents.

C is incorrect because the axes of a line graph show the independent and dependent variables.

D is correct because trends are shown on line graphs by lines of best fit that are based on data points.

5. B

A is incorrect because 60% of the 20 students earned a B or better. Sixty percent of 20 students would be 12 students, not 9 students.

B is correct because 60% of the 20 students earned a B or better. Sixty percent of 20 students would be 12 students.

C is incorrect because 60% of the 20 students earned a B or better. Sixty percent of 20 students would be 12 students, not 15 students.

D is incorrect because 60% of the 20 students earned a B or better. Sixty percent of 20 students would be 12 students, not 18 students.

Lesson 2 Quiz

1. A   4. A
2. B   5. C
3. D

1. A

A is correct because a computer is the only tool listed that can store data, display trends, generate models, and run simulations. All of these are necessary to track a hurricane.

B is incorrect because a hand lens helps scientists magnify things.

C is incorrect because an electron microscope magnifies very small objects.

D is incorrect because an MRI would not be used to track a hurricane.

2. B

A is incorrect because scientists do use approximate measurements (estimates).

B is correct because scientists use approximate measurements (estimates) to determine whether the data they collected is reasonable.

C is incorrect because scientists use digital cameras to accomplish the recording of objects or environments in a brief interval of time.

D is incorrect because various tools help scientists take measurements that cannot be detected by the senses alone.

3. D

A is incorrect because the SI was not developed to compete with any other measurement system.

B is incorrect because the SI enabled countries to use just one system.

C is incorrect because the SI was designed to allow scientists to share their scientific discoveries, not keep them secret.

D is correct because the SI was designed to allow scientists from everywhere to share data, observations, and measurements with other scientists.

4. A

A is correct because the measurements are close to the actual value (accurate), and they are far apart from one another (not precise).

B   is incorrect because the measurements are close to the actual value (accurate), and they are far apart from one another (not precise).

C   is incorrect because even though the measurements are close to the actual value (accurate), they are not near one another (precise).

D   is incorrect because the measurements are close to the center (accurate), even though they are not close to one another (precise).

5.   C

A   is incorrect because writing meters does not tell us the number in the measurement.

B   is incorrect because writing 10 does not tell us the unit in the measurement.

C   is correct because the answer includes the number and the unit in the correct order.

D   is incorrect because the measurement is not in order with the number first and the unit second.

Lesson 3 Quiz

1.   C   4.   D
2.   B   5.   B
3.   D

1.   C

A   is incorrect because a scale model is a smaller version of a physical model.

B   is incorrect because a physical model is a tangible model of some object.

C   is correct because a conceptual model is a representation of how parts of a system are related or organized.

D   is incorrect because a mathematical model would have numbers, equations, or other data.

2.   B

A   is incorrect because a system does not show what would happen in the case of a specific circumstance.

B   is correct because a simulation imitates an event and shows how an event would occur under specific circumstances.

C   is incorrect because a conceptual model represents how parts of a system are related or organized.

D   is incorrect because a mathematical model is usually made up of numbers, equations, or other data.

3.   D

A   is incorrect because a toy car is a physical model of a real car.

B   is incorrect because a miniature train is a tiny version of a real train.

C   is incorrect because a stuffed animal is a toy version of the real organism.

D   is correct because a chemical equation is a mathematical model.

4.   D

A   is incorrect because this answer describes why a physical model is used.

B   is incorrect because this answer describes the limitations of a physical model (objects).

C   is incorrect because this answer describes the limitations of a conceptual model (ideas)

D   is correct because this answer describes the limitations of a mathematical model (data, variables, and factors).

5.   B

A   is incorrect because a simulation imitates an event; it is not a model.

B   is correct because a scale model is used to study objects that are too big or too small to see.

C   is incorrect because a conceptual model deals with verbal or graphical explanations, not objects.

D   is incorrect because a mathematical model deals with equations and quantitative processes.

Lesson 1 Alternative Assessment

Model: Model shows the classroom and describes two advantages and two limitations of the model.

Table 1: Table shows the results of 100 coin tosses. Explanation tells how the data can be graphed.

Table 2: Table shows how many students in the class write with the left or right hand. Explanation tells how the data can be graphed.

Graph 1: Line graphs accurately present the data about average temperature each month for a year, and describe which month is the hottest and which is the coldest.

Graph 2: Line graphs accurately represent a car traveling 80 km/hr for 400 kilometers, and tell how long it would take the car to travel 360 kilometers.

Graph 3: Line graphs accurately show the average size of the ozone hole between the years 1979 and 1994. Students describe overall trends shown by the graph and explain why some data do not fit the trend.

Lesson 2 Alternative Assessment

Proper Tools: Students should mention that the proper tools used correctly assure that accurate data is collected. Some reasons why data might be inaccurate include using broken equipment, using the wrong tool, or using a tool incorrectly.

Conversion Factors: Students should report measurements made with the chosen, nonstandard unit and with a meterstick. Responses should also include an assessment of the accuracy of measurements made with the nonstandard unit.

Design an Experiment: Students should include the tools needed to perform the experiment. Students should also include a description of how the tools will be used.

Measurement Standards: Skits should include the following information: The International System of Units, or SI, was developed centuries ago to make it possible to compare measurements made by people in different locations using different tools. By using SI units, all scientists can share and com-pare their observations and results.

Measuring Length, Mass, Time and Temperature: Worksheets should include the following in-formation: length, ruler, meter; mass, balance, kilogram; time, stopwatch, second; temperature, thermometer, kelvin. An answer key should be provided for the worksheet.

Scientific Tools: Articles should be similar in style to a newspaper article, and should include the following information: Computers may be used to store, calculate, and use data, generate charts to display trends, and generate models or run simulations.

Lesson 3 Alternative Assessment

The specific advantages and limitations of the model: At least one specific advantage of using this model is described; at least one specific limitation of this model is described.

How the model can be used to make predictions: Student specifically describes how this model can be used to make predictions about the results of a process, the outcome of a test, or future conditions in a system.

A detailed description of the types of simulations the model could be utilized in: Response indicates an understanding of the concept that simulations utilize models, and clearly describes how the specific model could be used in a simulation.

A comparison of the model to the actual object, system, or process it represents: Specific similarities and differences between the model and the object, system, or process it represents are identified.

An explanation about what features make the model a physical, mathematical, or conceptual model: Response correctly classifies the model and identifies features and characteristics of the model that account for its classification.

Performance-Based Assessment

See Unit 2, Lesson 2

3. Answers may vary. Sample answer: The conversion factor is 4.7 paperclips to 1 pencil.

7. Answers may vary. Sample data table:

Data Table				
Object	Paper clip units	Pencil units*	Centi-meters	Meters *
Table	51	10.8	152	1.52
Chair	30	6.4	90	0.90
Student	41	8.7	122	1.22
Com-puter	14	3.0	43	0.43
Book	7	1.5	21	0.21
White board	29	6.2	87	0.87
Poster	28	6.0	85	0.85
Key board	15	3.1	44	0.44
Folder	12	2.6	37	0.37
Note book	7	1.5	21	0.21

*Calculate using conversion factor

8. Answers may vary. Sample answer: 20 minutes

10. Answers may vary. Sample answer: 10 minutes

11. Our own system of measurement took longer to convert the measurements. The metric system was faster.

12. The calculations to convert "paper clip" units into "pencil" units took longer because the calculations were more complicated. The metric system was faster because it simply required dividing by a factor of 10 to convert the measurements.

13. Answers may vary. Sample answer: Because the metric system is faster and simpler, it is a better system.

Unit Review

Vocabulary

1. **models** See Unit 2, Lesson 1

2. **measurement** See Unit 2, Lesson 2

3. **physical model** See Unit 2, Lesson 3

4. **independent variable** See Unit 2, Lesson 1

5. **simulations** See Unit 2, Lesson 3

Key Concepts

6. C	9. D	12. C
7. B	10. A	13. D
8. C	11. D	

6. C See Unit 2, Lesson 1

A is incorrect because the graph shows that the salary is decreased from the previous year in 2002, 2004, and 2008.

B is incorrect because the graph shows that the salary is decreased from the previous year in 2002, 2004, and 2008.

C is correct because the graph shows that the salary decreased three times: from 2001 to 2002, from 2003 to 2004, and from 2007 to 2008.

D is incorrect because the graph shows that the salary is decreased from the previous year in 2002, 2004, and 2008.

7. B See Unit 2, Lesson 1

A is incorrect because 1 shows a solid and 2 shows a liquid.

B is correct because the particles in the model are floating out of the container, and a gas does not hold the shape of a container.

C is incorrect because 2 shows a liquid.

D is incorrect because 1 shows a solid.

8. C See Unit 2, Lesson 2

A is incorrect because a pound is a non-SI unit of mass.

B is incorrect because a meter is a unit of length.

C is correct because the kilogram is the SI unit used to measure mass, and is used by scientists. Mass can be measured with an electronic balance.

D is incorrect because ounces are non-SI units of mass.

9. D See Unit 2, Lesson 2

A is incorrect because scientists use test tubes to hold samples of materials in the lab.

B is incorrect because scientists use hot plates to increase the temperature of a substance in the lab.

C is incorrect because scientists use electron microscopes to see more detail than with regular microscopes.

D is correct because a scientist would not usually use an object that measures in non-SI units.

10. A See Unit 2, Lesson 2

A is correct because scientific notation is a way of representing very long numbers in a short way.

B is incorrect because there is no stipulation about reporting data to the tenth decimal point.

C is incorrect because scientists do not need to use fractions when they report very large numbers.

D is incorrect because scientists would not report units in inches.

11. D See Unit 2, Lesson 3

A is incorrect because simulations imitate the function of the thing it is representing.

B is incorrect because a simulation imitates the behavior of whatever it is representing.

C is incorrect because a simulation imitates the process of what it is representing.

D is correct because the simulation cannot take the place of the process or thing it represents.

12. C See Unit 2, Lesson 3

A   is incorrect because a mathematical model is usually made up of numbers, equations or other forms of data.

B   is incorrect because a simulation would imitate the function, and this simply gives a picture of the process.

C   is correct because the rock cycle is a conceptual model of how parts of a system are related or organized.

D   is incorrect because a physical model represents the physical structure of a system, and the diagram does not do this.

13. D See Unit 2, Lesson 1

A   is incorrect because the entire line graph is for full–sun plants, and Emmanuel needs to include the plant height as one of the axes.

B   is incorrect because the conditions are full sun for the entire graph, in this case the conditions are "full sun".

C   is incorrect because the condition is full sun, so that condition would not change.

D   is correct because the graph would need to show the number of days over which the measurements were taken and the height of the plant on each day to show the growth of the plant in full sun.

Critical Thinking

14. See Unit 2, Lesson 2

- should include the knowledge that computers may be used to store, calculate, and use data, generate charts to display

trends, and generate models or run simulations

- may include knowledge that computers allow scientists to collect, interpret, and analyze data, as well as track data collected during long-term projects

15. See Unit 2, Lesson 1

- A scientific model is either a visual or mathematical representation of a scientific explanation.

- A disadvantage of using models might be that a certain model is not able to reproduce everything about the phenomenon it represents.

Connect Essential Questions

16. See Unit 2, Lesson 1 and Lesson 3

- A mathematical model is a mathematical representation of something occurring in the natural world.

- A conceptual model is a representation of how the parts of a system are related, how they work together, or how they are composed of objects or interactions in the natural world.

- An example of a mathematical model would be $E=mc^2$, which represents the idea that the mass of an object is a measure of the energy it contains. E is the energy of the object; m is mass, and c is the speed of light in a vacuum.

- An example of a conceptual model would be a food web,

which represents the predator-prey relationships in an ecosystem.

Unit Test A
Key Concepts

1. C   5. C   9. D
2. B   6. C   10. A
3. B   7. B   11. B
4. C   8. D   12. D

1. C

A   is incorrect because this number has only 13 places after the initial 5.

B   is incorrect because this number has only 19 places after the initial 5.

C   is correct because this number has 24 places after the initial 5.

D   is incorrect because this number has 27 places after the initial 5, 4 more than the correct number.

2. B

A   is incorrect because a hand lens would not magnify a cheek cell enough to see it clearly.

B   is correct because an electronic microscope is used to study microscopic things, like cells.

C   is incorrect because an MRI is too large-scale of a tool to use for a cheek cell.

D   is incorrect because a CAT scan is too large-scale of a tool to use for a cheek cell.

3. B

A   is incorrect because the hottest temperature (34 °C)

took place at 3:00 p.m., not
12:00 p.m. (noon).

B   is correct because the hottest
temperature (34 °C) took
place at 3:00 p.m.

C   is incorrect because the
hottest temperature (34 °C)
took place at 3:00 p.m., not
6:00 p.m.

D   is incorrect because the
hottest temperature (34 °C)
took place at 3:00 p.m., not
9:00 p.m.

4. C

A   is incorrect because about
35% of the circle graph is
shaded, which corresponds to
students who earned a C, not
an A.

B   is incorrect because about
35% of the circle graph is
shaded, which corresponds to
students who earned a C, not
a B.

C   is correct because about 35%
of the circle graph is shaded,
which corresponds to
students who earned a C.

D   is incorrect because about
35% of the circle graph is
shaded, which corresponds to
students who earned a C, not
a D.

5. C

A   is incorrect because a line
graph is not the most
effective graph for
representing percentages.

B   is incorrect because a scatter
plot is not the most effective
graph for representing
percentages.

C   is correct because a circle
graph is the most effective

graph for representing
percentages.

D   is incorrect because a box-
and-whisker plot is not the
most effective graph for
representing percentages.

6. C

A   is incorrect because time is
measured using a stopwatch.

B   is incorrect because length
can be measured using a
meter stick.

C   is correct because mass is not
measured with a graduated
cylinder, but with a balance,
triple beam balance or an
electronic balance.

D   is incorrect because
temperature is measured
using a thermometer.

7. B

A   is incorrect because a cell is
microscopic.

B   is correct because a real cell
is microscopic, and a model
lets the biologist teach the
class without needing
microscopes and other
equipment.

C   is incorrect because a real
cell is not necessarily too far
away to study.

D   is incorrect because a real
cell is not necessarily too
dangerous to study.

8. D

A   is incorrect because the
amount of vitamin C is the
independent variable, which
is being manipulated.

B   is incorrect because the
scientists are not testing the
type of illness.

C   is incorrect because the
scientists are not determining
what brand of vitamin C
works best.

D   is correct because the number
of illnesses may be dependent
on the amount of vitamin C
received, which makes it the
dependent variable.

9. D

A   is incorrect because a scale
model is appropriate for
physical objects. The board is
working with numbers.

B   is incorrect because a
physical model is appropriate
for physical objects. The
board is working with
numbers.

C   is incorrect because a
conceptual model is a
drawing, or a diagram, of a
process. The board is
working with numbers.

D   is correct because the board
is working with numbers, so
a mathematical model is most
appropriate.

10. A

A   is correct because the
measurements are both
accurate (the values are close
to the actual value) and
precise (each value is close to
all the other values
measured).

B   is incorrect because the
measurements are both
accurate (the values are close
to the actual value) and
precise (each value is close to
all the other values
measured).

C   is incorrect because the measurements are both accurate (the values are close to the actual value) and precise (each value is close to all the other values measured).

D   is incorrect because the measurements are both accurate (the values are close to the actual value) and precise (each value is close to all the other values measured).

11. B

A   is incorrect because quantitative situations are an advantage of using a mathematical model.

B   is correct because a scale model is a type of physical model, and a scale model is appropriate because a shopping mall is too large to see otherwise.

C   is incorrect because patterns of behavior are an advantage of using a mathematical model.

D   is incorrect because a conceptual model is appropriate for an abstract process that cannot be studied directly.

12. D

A   is incorrect because data and variables are a limitation of mathematical models.

B   is incorrect because ideas are a limitation of conceptual models.

C   is incorrect because the exclusion of factors is a

limitation of mathematical models.

D   is correct because a model not behaving like it should is a limitation of physical models.

Critical Thinking
13.

• description of geocentric model (e.g., *The geocentric model shows the other planets and the sun rotating around Earth*; etc.)

• description of heliocentric model (e.g., *The heliocentric model shows Earth and the other planets rotating about the sun*; etc.)

Extended Response
14.

• explanation of why an estimate was necessary (e.g., *Scientists estimated the gallons of oil spilled because it is not feasible to get an accurate measure in such a large body of water; Different groups of scientists used different tools; New observations were introduced into the data at different times*; etc.)

• a computer

• explanation of how a simulation would be useful (e.g., *A simulation would show how the oil spread initially; a simulation would predict how the oil might spread in the future*; etc.)

• description of limitations of tools to study oil spill (e.g., *Scientists are limited because these tools cannot measure the exact volume of oil spilled; these*

tools cannot reproduce everything about the oil spill; when dealing with a fluid substance such as water, tools can often have errors because things change so abruptly; etc.)

Unit Test B
Key Concepts
1. A   5. C   9. C
2. C   6. B   10. C
3. D   7. B   11. D
4. C   8. A   12. A

1. A

A   is correct because in scientific notation, every number after the decimal is counted as a decimal place. There are 24 places after the decimal in this number.

B   is incorrect because in scientific notation, every number after the decimal is counted as a decimal place. There are 24 places after the decimal in this number.

C   is incorrect because in scientific notation, every number after the decimal is counted as a decimal place. There are 24 places after the decimal in this number.

D   is incorrect because in scientific notation, every number after the decimal is counted as a decimal place. There are 24 places after the decimal in this number.

2. C

A   is incorrect because a hot plate is used to heat things.

B   is incorrect because a test tube is used to store substances.

C   is correct because an electronic balance is used to measure mass.

D   is incorrect because an electron microscope is used to study small things, like cells.

3. D

A   is incorrect because the coldest temperature was 17 °C, and the warmest temperature was 34 °C. This is a difference of 17 °C, not 7 °C.

B   is incorrect because the coldest temperature was 17 °C, and the warmest temperature was 34 °C. This is a difference of 17 °C, not 11 °C.

C   is incorrect because the coldest temperature was 17 °C, and the warmest temperature was 34 °C. This is a difference of 17 °C, not 13 °C.

D   is correct because the coldest temperature was 17 °C, and the warmest temperature was 34 °C. This is a difference of 17 °C.

4. C

A   is incorrect because the shaded wedge is larger than a quarter of the pie, so it is larger than 15%.

B   is incorrect because the shaded wedge is larger than a quarter of the pie, so it is larger than 25%.

C   is correct because the shaded wedge is larger than a quarter of the pie and smaller than half the pie. The answer

choice that corresponds to this range is 35%.

D   is incorrect because the shaded wedge is smaller than half of the pie, so it is less than 50%.

5. C

A   is incorrect because a line graph would be the most effective way to represent changes in temperature throughout a month.

B   is incorrect because a scatter plot would be the most effective way to represent the number of questions answered correctly by each student in a class.

C   is correct because a circle graph is the most effective graph for representing pieces of a whole, such as the percentages of a total budget.

D   is incorrect because a scatter plot would be the most effective way to represent the different heights reached by pea plants in an experiment.

6. B

A   is incorrect because length can be measured using a meter stick.

B   is correct because time is measured using a stopwatch or a clock. A graduated cylinder is used to measure volume.

C   is incorrect because temperature is measured using a thermometer.

D   is incorrect because mass is measured with a balance, triple beam balance or an electronic balance.

7. B

A   is incorrect because a scale model is a physical model that helps a scientist study the physical features of a volcano.

B   is correct because the scientist wants to make a prediction about a future event. Many different variables affect when a volcano will erupt, and a computer model would most effectively work with these variables to help the scientist make a reasonable prediction.

C   is incorrect because a physical model helps a scientist study the physical features of a volcano.

D   is incorrect because a diagram is a two-dimensional physical model that helps a scientist study the physical features of a volcano.

8. A

A   is correct because the amount of vitamin C is the independent variable, which is being manipulated.

B   is incorrect because the scientists are not determining what brand of vitamin C works best.

C   is incorrect because the scientists are not testing the type of illness.

D   is incorrect because the number of illnesses may be dependent on the amount of vitamin C received.

9. C

A   is incorrect because a scale model is appropriate for

physical objects. The board is working with a set of tasks or processes.

B   is incorrect because a physical model is appropriate for physical objects. The board is working with a set of tasks or processes.

C   is correct because a conceptual model is a drawing or a diagram of a process. The board is working with a set of tasks or processes, so a conceptual model is most appropriate.

D   is incorrect because a mathematical model is appropriate for numbers. The board is working with a set of tasks or processes.

10. C

A   is incorrect because the measurements are not accurate (the values are not close to the actual value), but they are precise (each value is close to all the other values measured).

B   is incorrect because the measurements are not accurate (the values are not close to the actual value), but they are precise (each value is close to all the other values measured).

C   is correct because the measurements are not accurate (the values are not close to the actual value), but they are precise (each value is close to all the other values measured).

D   is incorrect because the measurements are not accurate (the values are not

close to the actual value), but they are precise (each value is close to all the other values measured).

11. D

A   is incorrect because a scale model is a type of physical model that's appropriate to show objects that are too large to see.

B   is incorrect because patterns of behavior are an advantage of using a mathematical model.

C   is incorrect because a map is a type of physical model that's appropriate to show the layout of an place.

D   is correct because a conceptual model is appropriate for an abstract process that cannot be studied directly.

12. A

A   is correct because data and variables are a limitation of mathematical models.

B   is incorrect because ideas are a limitation of conceptual models.

C   is incorrect because size limitations can affect physical models.

D   is incorrect because a model not behaving like it should is a limitation of physical models.

Critical Thinking
13.

• explanation on why the geocentric model was rejected in favor of the heliocentric model (e.g., *New evidence was*

introduced that proved Earth rotated around the sun; new technology allowed scientists to make more accurate observations of the solar system; etc.).

Extended Response
14.

• explanation of an estimate and why estimates vary (e.g., *Scientists estimated the gallons of oil spilled because they needed to determine whether the data they collected was reasonable; scientists needed to decide what tool to use to measure the volume of the oil spill; different groups of scientists used different tools; new observations were introduced into the data at different times*; etc.)

• a computer

• a simulation

• description of limitations of tools for studying oil in the Gulf (e.g., *Scientists are limited because these tools cannot measure the exact volume of oil spilled; the tools cannot reproduce everything about the oil spill; when dealing with a fluid substance such as water, tools can often have errors because things change so abruptly*; etc.)

Unit 3 Engineering, Technology and Society
Unit Pretest

1. C	5. B	9. B
2. C	6. B	10. A
3. C	7. C	
4. B	8. A	

1. C

A   is incorrect because a metal has high density and high conductivity.

B   is incorrect because a ceramic has low conductivity, but it is brittle.

C   is correct because a polymer is made up of small molecules that link together to form larger molecules. Polymers typically have low density and conductivity.

D   is incorrect because a semiconductor is a compound with moderate conductivity.

2. C

A   is incorrect because Jacob would not use a system to help him decide what to bring to school.

B   is incorrect because Jacob would not use a test model to help him decide what to bring to school.

C   is correct because a Pugh chart can accommodate all of these variables and help Jacob decide what to bring to school.

D   is incorrect because there is no such tool as a trade-off table.

3. C

A   is incorrect because the image shows the scientists with a test model, or prototype, and prototypes are built after needs have been identified.

B   is incorrect because a test model is a prototype.

C   is correct because the image shows the scientists with a test model, or prototype, but there is no indication that the scientists have communicated their results to others.

D   is incorrect because the image shows the scientists with a test model, or prototype, and prototypes are built after solutions have been brainstormed.

4. B

A   is incorrect because engineers most use technology, science, and mathematics to solve real-world problems.

B   is correct because engineers most use technology, science, and mathematics to solve real-world problems.

C   is incorrect because engineers most use technology, science, and mathematics to solve real-world problems.

D   is incorrect because engineers most use technology, science, and mathematics to solve real-world problems.

5. B

A   is incorrect because the bacteria are being used to perform a technological process, not to create a new technology.

B   is correct because the bacteria are being used to treat wastewater, a technological application.

C   is incorrect because the bacteria are not new or changed by technology.

D   is incorrect because a technology was not applied to the bacteria; rather, the bacteria were used to perform a task.

6. B

A   is incorrect because the cycle of events is not a type of manual control.

B   is correct because with increases in carbon dioxide, Earth will eventually get warmer and warmer. This is an example of a positive feedback loop.

C   is incorrect because if the increase in carbon dioxide were an example of negative feedback, temperatures would cool after the rise in carbon dioxide.

D   is incorrect because the cycle of events is not a type of automatic control.

7. C

A   is incorrect because the student does not need a cyber tool such as a computer to measure a wooden board.

B   is incorrect because a complex tool is unnecessary to perform a simple task such as measuring a wooden board.

C   is correct because a physical tool, such as a meterstick, would be the best choice.

D   is incorrect because a composite is a classification of a type of material, not a type of tool.

8. A

A   is correct because scientists want to maximize the expected and favorable effects of technology, and minimize the unexpected and unfavorable effects.

B is incorrect because scientists try to minimize the expected unfavorable effects.

C is incorrect because although an unexpected favorable effect is good, scientists still try to minimize the number of unexpected effects of technology.

D is incorrect because scientists try to minimize the unexpected and unfavorable effects.

9. B

A is incorrect because this is not an image of the natural world but the designed, human-built world.

B is correct because the buildings, cars, and street all indicate the world designed by humans.

C is incorrect because even though science helped build this world, this is not the scientific world.

D is incorrect because even though components of this image are mechanical (cars), other components, such as buildings and roads, are not.

10. A

A is correct because the evidence suggests that the authorities blocked the vaccine based on cultural reasons: a preference for population growth.

B is incorrect because the passage makes no mention of economic issues.

C is incorrect because the vaccine was the technology that the authorities were

deciding on, not the deciding factor.

D is incorrect because the passage makes no mention of environmental concerns.

Lesson 1 Quiz

1. D   4. C
2. B   5. D
3. B

1. D

A is incorrect because creative thinking is an important skill for an engineer.

B is incorrect because methodical thinking is an important skill for an engineer.

C is incorrect because using math and models is a technical skill that would be required for designing a bridge.

D is correct because designing a controlled experiment is a skill that scientists use, but would not be used by engineers when designing a bridge.

2. B

A is incorrect because reporting the results is the last step in the engineering design process.

B is correct because these steps are in the correct order in the engineering design process.

C is incorrect because building and testing a prototype comes after a need has been identified and the research has been conducted.

D is incorrect because carrying out research is the second part after identifying a need.

3. B

A is incorrect because although a model is a type of reproduction of the actual product, a prototype is an initial test model of a product.

B is correct because a prototype is a test model of a product.

C is incorrect because a computer is not a first test motel.

D is incorrect because an application is a technological component.

4. C

A is incorrect because science is the study of the natural world.

B is incorrect because technology is the application of science for practical purposes.

C is correct because engineering is the application of science and mathematics to solve real-life problems.

D is incorrect because technology is the use of tools, machines, materials, and processes to meet human needs.

5. D

A is incorrect because engineering also includes mathematics.

B is incorrect because engineering also includes technology.

C is incorrect because engineering also includes science.

D is correct because engineering combines all three: science, technology, and mathematics.

Lesson 2 Quiz

1. A   4. D
2. A   5. C
3. D

1. A

A is correct because a technology would most likely be adopted if its benefits outweigh its risks.

B is incorrect because a technology would not likely be adopted if its risks outweigh its benefits.

C is incorrect because a technology almost always has a risk associated with it. The crucial question is whether the risks outweigh the benefits.

D is incorrect because a technology almost always has a benefit associated with it. The crucial question is whether the risks outweigh the benefits.

2. A

A is correct because the example depicts a trade-off: less data storage for longer battery life.

B is incorrect because life-cycle analyses focus on materials, energy, transportation, sale, use, and disposal of technology.

C is incorrect because the example is not a technological breakthrough.

D is incorrect because a method may lead to an effect, but it is not equivalent to an effect.

3. D

A is incorrect because a life-cycle analysis is not used to decide whether to use a risk-benefit analysis.

B is incorrect because a life-cycle analysis is not used to decide whether to test a technology.

C is incorrect because a life-cycle analysis is not used to compare technology.

D is correct because a life-cycle analysis is often used to determine the total lifetime cost of a technology.

4. D

A is incorrect because a robot that short circuits and then catches fire is not favorable.

B is incorrect because a robot that short circuits and then catches fire is not favorable, even though it was unexpected.

C is incorrect because the researchers were surprised, thus this is not an expected effect.

D is correct because the researchers are surprised that the robot caught fire, making it unexpected. By catching fire, the event is also unfavorable because the robot is supposed to be fire resistant.

5. C

A is incorrect because a trade-off is not a table.

B is incorrect because a prototype is a test model, not a table.

C is correct because this type of table is a Pugh chart containing a product and criteria to determine which backpack to use.

D is incorrect because a risk-benefit analysis may take the form of a table, but this table does not weigh risks and benefits.

Lesson 3 Quiz

1. D   4. B
2. D   5. A
3. A

1. D

A is incorrect because a sprinkler system is usually automatic because people must evacuate buildings in the case of a fire.

B is incorrect because a manual control would require someone to remain in the building to engage the sprinkler system, which is dangerous in the event of a fire.

C is incorrect because positive feedback is a component of a control system but would not be used for a sprinkler system.

D is correct because a sprinkler system is usually automatic for reasons of safety and ease of use.

2. D

A is incorrect because systems are considered distinct physical entities for the purpose of study.

B is incorrect because systems do have inputs and outputs.

C is incorrect because systems do have processes that take place within the system itself.

D is correct because a system's components do not work independently of one another; rather, they interact.

3. A

A is correct because interconnected systems are systems that interact with each other; therefore, changing one system will have an effect on the other system.

B is incorrect because interconnected systems are systems that interact with each other, but a change in one part of one system may have no effect on the same part of the other system.

C is incorrect because interconnected systems are systems that interact with each other, but an improvement to one system may have a very different effect on the other system.

D is incorrect because interconnected systems are systems that interact with each other, but there is no necessary connection between positive feedback from one system and negative feedback from the other system.

4. B

A is incorrect because an input is added to a system, but in this image, the person is

taking paper away from the printer.

B is correct because an input is added to a system; in this image, the person is entering data into a computer by typing on a keyboard.

C is incorrect because an input is added to a system, but in this image, the person is passively watching television.

D is incorrect because an input is added to a system; in this image, the person is cleaning the computer screen, but not actually adding anything to the computer system.

5. A

A is correct because a control regulates a system.

B is incorrect because a person studying a system might organize a system's components.

C is incorrect because a system that does not interact with the outside environment is a closed system.

D is incorrect because a control does not transform negative feedback into positive feedback.

Lesson 4 Quiz

1. A   4. A
2. B   5. C
3. D

1. A

A is correct because a software program, or cyber tool, on a computer, could map an otherwise inaccessible area such as the ocean floor.

B is incorrect because a computer is a physical tool, but without the proper software, or cyber tool, the computer would not be able to create a map of the ocean floor.

C is incorrect because ceramic is a type of material with no clear connection to ocean-floor mapping.

D is incorrect because creating a map of the ocean floor does not require taking a chemical analysis.

2. B

A is incorrect because a hammer is not a cyber tool. A cyber tool is software, which is necessary for computers to operate.

B is correct because a hammer is a type of physical tool.

C is incorrect because a hammer is a physical tool that may be made partly with polymers, but it is not a polymer material.

D is incorrect because a hammer is a physical tool that may be made partly with composite material, but it is not a composite material.

3. D

A is incorrect because physical tools may be used in the modification and study of materials, but they do not represent the use of materials science.

B is incorrect because cyber tools may be used in the modification and study of materials, but they do not represent the use of materials science.

C is incorrect because the actual building of an automobile does not represent the use of materials science.

D is correct because the creation of steel, a stronger alloy that can be used for a variety of purposes, is an example of the use of materials science. The creation of steel has allowed for new technologies and thus, growth of technology.

4. A

A is correct because a composite material is made of two or more materials combined together. Ceramics can be, but are not always, made up of two or more combined materials.

B is incorrect because a polymer is a large molecule made of smaller molecules.

C is incorrect because a metal is made out of metallic elements held together by a metallic bond.

D is incorrect because a semiconductor is a material with moderate electrical conductivity and low thermal conductivity.

5. C

A is incorrect because cost can be related to the availability of a material, but in this situation, cost is not specifically mentioned.

B is incorrect because flexibility refers to the quality

or classification of a material; it is not necessarily a limit.

C is correct because a material that is difficult to obtain is unavailable.

D is incorrect because a material may be difficult to obtain for many reasons other than its degree of hazard.

Lesson 5 Quiz

1. D   4. A
2. B   5. A
3. C

1. D

A is incorrect because this is an example of a product created from the silk a spider produces.

B is incorrect because this is an example of a product created from the genetic composition of bacteria.

C is incorrect because this is an example of a product created from a material made by barnacles.

D is correct because an airplane wing is an example of a product created by copying the structure of a bird's wing.

2. B

A is incorrect because a medical procedure is used to diagnose or treat disease, not a technology used to improve vision.

B is correct because an assistive technology is a physical object that helps a living thing with life processes such as seeing clearly.

C is incorrect because a medicine is a chemical product that helps a living

thing fight disease or regulate bodily functions.

D is incorrect because eyeglasses do not modify a person's genes.

3. C

A is incorrect because a product is not being designed, but rather an organism (tomato plant) is being genetically modified by injecting genes into the tomato to produce a favorable trait, such as cold weather resistance.

B is incorrect because selective breeding relies on emphasizing a favorable natural variation or desirable traits by cross-breeding or cross-pollination and not necessarily injecting fluids.

C is correct because the scientist is injecting genes into the organism to modify the organism's genetic makeup.

D is incorrect because the production of a medicine is not the likeliest process being shown through the injection of a tomato with a needle.

4. A

A is correct because technology can change living things through selective breeding and genetic modification.

B is incorrect because organisms, such as yeast and bacteria, can be a type of technology.

C is incorrect because living things can inspire new technologies, such as the design technology of swimsuit fabric from sharks skin and helicopter wings from dragonflies.

D is incorrect because technology can help living things carry out life processes. For example, eyeglasses help people to see clearly.

5. A

A is correct because yeast is a living organism that is used to make bread.

B is incorrect because gasoline is a fossil fuel that forms from the decay of organisms that lived thousands of years ago.

C is incorrect because prosthetics are mechanical limbs that are sometimes modeled on the limbs of living organisms, but living organisms are not used to make prosthetics.

D is incorrect because airplane wings are sometimes modeled on the wings of living organisms, but living organisms are not used to make airplane wings.

Lesson 6 Quiz

1. B   4. A
2. D   5. B
3. D

1. B

A is incorrect because technology typically leads to changes in the natural order.

B is correct because technology is developed to meet people's needs and wants.

C is incorrect because technologies often lead to the development of new technology, but often old technology is improved rather than replaced completely.

D is incorrect because one of the main goals of technology is to make society more efficient.

2. D

A is incorrect because even though we make a trade-off through the use of cars, smog itself has negative consequences.

B is incorrect because social norms help guide the actions of people in a society.

C is incorrect because smog has negative consequences such as acid rain, so it is not a positive effect.

D is correct because smog is a negative effect; it is a type of air pollution.

3. D

A is incorrect because the compact disc with greater storage capacity was a more useful means of storage.

B is incorrect because the floppy disk was not used to create a new need or want; the original need of storing data was improved through the development of the compact disc.

C is incorrect because the floppy disk was not used to develop the designed world.

D is correct because floppy disks led to the development of newer compact discs.

4. A

A is correct because technology is usually chosen by looking at the trade-offs between environmental concerns, economic issues, and cultural practices, beliefs, and norms.

B is incorrect because these three examples are not trade-offs; they are parts of the technological process.

C is incorrect because these three examples are separate components, not trade-offs.

D is incorrect because these three examples are components of technology and engineering.

5. B

A is incorrect because the natural world is not designed by engineers, scientists, or technologists.

B is correct because the collection of technological systems is known as the designed world.

C is incorrect because technological systems incorporate more than just the life science world.

D is incorrect because materials science concerns materials and how to utilize them.

Lesson 1 Alternative Assessment

The End of Papers? Essays reflect an understanding of the concept that successful technologies meet a need. Essays are clearly written and use examples and evidence to support argument.

Mobile: Finished mobiles should be in equilibrium, with all parts balanced. Presentations should include detailed description of design flaws and how they were dealt with.

Underwater Lab: Proposals should provide logical justifications for using a certain type of prototype.

Adaptive Devices: Posters present a range of adaptive devices and use images and captions to demonstrate how the devices solve everyday problems.

Constraints: Lists identify four or more constraints, such as cost, size of pieces (small pieces could be swallowed), toxicity of materials, and durability of materials.

Job Description: Job descriptions clearly identify specific engineering design skills and areas of scientific knowledge (such as chemistry) needed for the job.

Lesson 2 Alternative Assessment

The expected, unexpected, favorable, and unfavorable effects of the technology: Effects of the technology are identified and classified as expected, unexpected, favorable, or unfavorable.

Trade-offs associated with the manufacture or use of the product: Student identifies at least one specific risk or disadvantage that is accepted in exchange for a benefit of the technology; or clearly identifies one benefit of the technology that

is given up to gain another benefit of the technology.

Risk-benefit analysis of the use of the technology: Unfavorable effects and favorable effects of the technology are compared in a two-column table or other organized way.

Life cycle analysis of the technology from production through disposal: Specific economic and environmental effects of the production, use, and disposal of the technology are identified.

Pugh chart comparing the technology to other similar technologies: Pugh carts include several forms of technology listed in the left column of the chart, and include features of the technologies compared in the rows of the chart.

Lesson 3 Alternative Assessment

The system's input, output, and method of control: The inputs and outputs for the system are clearly described, and include not only materials, but also inputs and outputs such as energy and information. The function of each type of input should be described. The method or methods of control should be identified and described. Each control type should be identified as manual or automatic. Presentation identifies by description or labels the flow of inputs and outputs.

The system's feedback methods and interactions with other systems: All feedback mechanisms used by the system should be clearly described,

including how the feedback might affect the system. Systems with which the system interactions should be identified and clearly described. Presentation identifies by description or labels how feedback affects the system and how the system interacts with other systems.

The system's effectiveness and ways to make the system work better: Whether or not the system operates effectively and why or why not should be clearly described. Ideas for increasing the system's effectiveness should be clearly described. Presentation identifies through description or labels areas in which the system could be made more effective.

Lesson 4 Alternative Assessment

Explain how testing is important for tools and materials: Demonstrate knowledge that testing tools and materials prior to use identifies flaws and properties that are not as predicted. It is also cheaper to test a material or prototype before large-scale use.

Compare properties of two or more materials: Through testing or research, reach conclusions about the similarities and differences between properties of materials, such as conductivity, malleability, ductility, melting point, strength, or hardness.

Relate properties of materials with their uses: Demonstrate understanding, using examples, that the properties of materials make them desirable for some uses and less functional for others.

Describe how new tools improve materials: Provide an example of how new tools for testing or altering materials, as well as cyber tools for predicting outcomes, can lead to improved materials or new uses of existing materials.

Describe how new materials improve tools: Provide examples of how a new material has made a technological product work better, faster, or more efficiently.

Explain how new tools and materials impact people and society: Provide examples of how a new tool or material has helped people or changed the way people do things.

Identify a problem and how materials science provides a solution: Describe a problem, past or present, that materials science has helped solve, or may help solve in the future.

Lesson 5 Alternative Assessment

Biomimicry: Sketches feature a technological design for a new invention, and state how two features of the design were inspired by the features of a flying squirrel.

Company Brochure: Brochures include an overview and examples of the four key topics: biotechnology, genetic technology, medical technology, and biomimicry.

Executive Chef: Recipes include an ingredient list and a written description, drawing, or

photograph of the finished product that details how biotechnology is used to produce at least three of the ingredients.

Then to Now: Timelines use at least three pictures and visuals to illustrate changes in the technology over a period of time.

Trading Cards: Cards illustrate and describe at least five organisms that are related to engineering and technology, including an example of selective breeding and genetic engineering.

Crazier Glue: Packaging for the product describes and markets synthetic barnacle glue, including how it is an example of biomimicry.

Amazing Bacteria: Print or digital skits PSA dispel common misconceptions about bacteria, and introduces ways bacteria are useful biotechnology in everyday life and through genetic modification.

Cat's Meow: Press releases detail the sequence of steps involved in genetic engineering and clearly state one application of this genetic modification in a cat.

Film Crew: Skits illustrate four activities or topics that are examples of how engineering and technology are related to life science.

Lesson 6 Alternative Assessment

Examples: A specific form of technology is identified, and at least ten specific effects of this technology are listed. Student

includes an opinion of each effect, either positive or negative.

Illustrations: Collage includes images associated with engineering, technology, and society. Each image is accompanied by a caption that states how the image shows the relationship between engineering, technology, and society.

Analysis: A reasoned response to the question is offered, including specific examples that were considered when developing the response.

Observations: Presentation clearly shows the effects of a technology on the student's life.

Models: Diagram clearly models the two-way relationship between technology and society.

Performance-Based Assessment

See Unit 3, Lesson 4

8. Answers may vary. Students may notice smell, color, thickness, and other characteristics.

9. Answers may vary.

10. Answers may vary. Sample answer: Wood glue changed the color of the tissue paper. Epoxy made the sponge brittle.

11. Answers may vary.

Unit Review
Vocabulary

1. **C See Unit 3, Lesson 1**
2. **A See Unit 3, Lesson 1**
3. **D See Unit 3, Lesson 2**
4. **B See Unit 3, Lesson 2**
5. **A See Unit 3, Lesson 3**

Key Concepts

6. A	10. B	14. A
7. C	11. B	15. D
8. D	12. A	16. A
9. C	13. C	

6. A See Unit 3, Lesson 1

A is correct because technology is used to develop practical products and processes.

B is incorrect because the statement describes engineering.

C is incorrect because the statement describes science.

D is incorrect because the statement describes the philosophy of science.

7. C See Unit 3, Lesson 6

A is incorrect because Krisha and her friends had been using the phones before the trouble began.

B is incorrect because the phones were new and based on new phone technology.

C is correct because the technology could have such unintended negative effects as overloading a phone system.

D is incorrect because the phones were based on new cell phone technology.

8. D See Unit 3, Lesson 2

A is incorrect because a list of building materials would be created after the location was chosen.

B is incorrect because a life cycle analysis evaluates the materials and energy used to build, sell, use, and dispose of the housing.

C is incorrect because creating a model of senior citizen housing would not help in choosing a location.

D is correct because knowing earthquake risks is an important part of making a decision about location.

9. C See Unit 3, Lesson 2

A is incorrect because computer programs are complex tools used in design.

B is incorrect because an electron microscope is a complex tool that can be used to evaluate or analyze.

C is correct because a suspension bridge is not a tool, it is a result of engineering design and building technology.

D is incorrect because a power drill is a simple tool that can be used to create a technological product.

10. B See Unit 3, Lesson 2

A is incorrect because the illustration does not show data related to traffic jams.

B is correct because the exhaust gases from the internal combustion engines of automobiles are waste products that contain air pollutants.

C is incorrect because the illustration does not contain data related to accidents.

D is incorrect because the illustration does not contain data about increased jobs and other benefits.

11. B See Unit 3, Lesson 4

A is incorrect because metals are made of metallic elements from the periodic table.

B is correct because cement is a ceramic material, a nonmetal made up of inorganic minerals.

C is incorrect because polymers are large molecules used to make such materials as plastics.

D is incorrect because semiconductors are weak conductors of electricity commonly used in computer chips and other electronic products.

12. A See Unit 3, Lesson 4

A is correct because the data in the chart show a material's ability to control the flow of thermal energy.

B is incorrect because plastic foam and ceramic are not composites.

C is incorrect because the chart does not provide any data on the material's strength.

D is incorrect because the data does not give information about weight to strength.

13. C See Unit 3, Lesson 5

A is incorrect because selective breeding involves breeding individuals with desired traits.

B is incorrect because it is the goal of scientists, not engineers, to learn more about nature.

C is correct because genetic engineering involves inserting genes from one organism into the DNA of another organism.

D is incorrect because scientists and engineers must have already modeled what DNA looks like in order to cut the strand at a particular place.

14. A See Unit 3, Lesson 5

A is correct because a cardboard shipping box is not similar to anything used in nature.

B is incorrect because the wings of birds inspired wings for airplanes.

C is incorrect because the human hormone insulin, which controls blood sugar, was made into a drug for treating diabetes.

D is incorrect because the webbed feet of animals, such as frogs, inspired flippers for swimming.

15. D See Unit 3, Lesson 6

A is incorrect because the need for lighting was related to dark rooms, not the height of buildings.

B is incorrect because streets paving and building height are not related.

C is incorrect because communications technology is related to sending messages over a distance.

D is correct because the more floors a building contained, the more difficult it was to walk to the upper floors.

16. A See Unit 3, Lesson 1

A is correct because the natural wind speed and direction were variables outside the

control of engineers, and the prototype could not gather this type of information.

B is incorrect because engineers could determine the needed amount of electricity and calculate the blade speed that would generate this amount of electricity.

C is incorrect because the prototype could indicate how fast the blades turned in different wind speeds.

D is incorrect because the prototype could indicate the level of sound from the blades turning at high speed.

Critical Thinking

17. See Unit 3, Lesson 3

Answers may vary. Sample answer:

• *Taking the lid off of the pot would create an open system.*

• *Replacing the lid, or leaving the lid on the pot would create a closed system)*

• *An open system freely exchanges energy and matter with its surroundings, but a closed system exchanges only energy with its surroundings. In the closed system, the water molecules (matter) are remaining in the pot, and only thermal energy is moving out of the pot. In the open system both thermal energy and water molecules are leaving the pot.*

18. See Unit 3, Lesson 6

Answers may vary. Sample answer:

• *People's health improved because food did not spoil so*

quickly due to microorganisms, and people did not have to shop as often for milk, eggs, and other groceries. Medicines and other temperature sensitive materials can be stored and transported to places of need without spoilage.

• *Frozen meats, frozen vegetables and whole dinners. Ice cream and other frozen treats (ice pops, frozen yogurt, etc.).*

19. See Unit 3, Lesson 3

Answers may vary. Sample answer:

• *A thermostat is a sensor.*

• *The thermostat senses changes in temperature, which serves as feedback about how the system is operating.*

• *When the temperature falls below a certain set point on the thermostat, the furnace turns on to supply more thermal energy.*

Connect Essential Questions

20. See Unit 3, Lesson 1, Lesson 2, Lesson 4, and Lesson 6

Answers may vary. Sample answer:

• *The increasing difficulty of drilling for oil used to make jet fuel created a need to transport people more efficiently.*

• *The material for an airplane would need to be strong, lightweight, and easily shaped.*

- *Airlines might have to charge passengers more for tickets or the passenger seats might be made of less expensive material.*

- *The steps for improving a material for airplane wings and bodies begins by identifying what is needed in a new material, conducting research to learn more about the problem and whether others have tried solutions, brainstorming solutions with a group, building, testing, and evaluating a prototype material, improving the prototype, and communicating the results.*

Unit Test A
Key Concepts

1. D	6. C	11. C
2. A	7. C	12. B
3. C	8. D	13. D
4. C	9. B	14. A
5. A	10. C	15. A

1. D

A is incorrect because material A is a metal.

B is incorrect because material B is a ceramic.

C is incorrect because material C is a polymer.

D is correct because material D is a composite.

2. A

A is correct because a city is the best example of the designed world, because a city contains little of the natural world and many objects designed by scientists, technologists, and engineers.

B is incorrect because compared to a city, a park is much less designed.

C is incorrect because compared to a city and park, a rural town is less designed.

D is incorrect because compared to a city, park, and rural town, the countryside is the least designed.

3. C

A is incorrect because airbags are an example of technology changing to become safer.

B is incorrect because cell phones that feature different colors, shapes, and ring tones are examples of technology changing to create new wants.

C is correct because smaller computers that can perform more operations are more efficient than their larger, slower predecessors.

D is incorrect because solar cells are examples of technology changing in response to the problem of polluting, nonrenewable energy resources.

4. C

A is incorrect because the images do not show the train or the bird moving, so the images do not justify conclusions about the relative speeds of either the train or the bird.

B is incorrect because the images do not show the materials used to make the train or the materials found in the kingfisher's ecosystem,

so comparisons between these materials are unjustified.

C is correct because the shapes of the kingfisher's beak and the bullet train's nose are almost identical, which suggests the technology was inspired by nature.

D is incorrect because the shape of the bird's beak came first; the bullet train was most likely inspired by the beak.

5. A

A is correct because creating a prototype would most likely occur during the research phase.

B is incorrect because a prototype would not be created during the testing phase; it would be tested.

C is incorrect because a prototype would be created after the problem was identified or defined.

D is incorrect because a prototype would need to be created before the scientists could communicate the results of the test.

6. C

A is incorrect because the invention of the radio and television is a better example of how new technology often drives the development of newer technology.

B is incorrect because the discovery of new planets and stars, although important for the science of astronomy, does not have a direct effect on society on Earth.

C is correct because the movement of people away from cities and to suburbs and more remote locations changes society for the people who move as well as for the people who do not move.

D is incorrect because sign language is not an example of technology.

7. C

A is incorrect because playing sports is not a life process.

B is incorrect because accessing the Internet is not a life process.

C is correct because moving one's body is a life process, and a wheelchair can help a person move his or her body.

D is incorrect because attending class is not a life process.

8. D

A is incorrect because a car has a value of 8, making it a better option to choose than walking.

B is incorrect because a train has a value of 5, making it a better option than walking a distance of 200 miles.

C is incorrect because an airplane has a value of 8, making it a better option to choose than walking.

D is correct because walking has a value of 3, and is only better than the other options in terms of cost. Walking is the least desirable way to travel 200 miles.

9. B

A is incorrect because this is a trade-off in which the benefit of turning up the heat

(increased comfort) is sacrificed to minimize a harmful effect (air pollution caused by generating electricity).

B is correct because this is a trade-off in which the benefit of turning up the heat (increased comfort) is sacrificed to minimize a harmful effect (air pollution caused by generating electricity).

C is incorrect because this is a trade-off in which the benefit of turning up the heat (increased comfort) is sacrificed to minimize a harmful effect (air pollution caused by generating electricity).

D is incorrect because this is a trade-off in which the benefit of turning up the heat (increased comfort) is sacrificed to minimize a harmful effect (air pollution caused by generating electricity).

10. C

A is incorrect because a printer outputs data from a computer

B is incorrect because a speaker outputs sound from a computer.

C is correct because a keyboard is a device that inputs data into a computer.

D is incorrect because headphones are another source of output from a computer.

11. C

A is incorrect because when systems are interconnected, a

change in one system causes a change in the other system; in this example, the shower does not cause another technological system to change.

B is incorrect because when systems are interconnected, a change in one system causes a change in the other system; in this example, the bicycle does not cause another technological system to change.

C is correct because when systems are interconnected, a change in one system causes a change in the other system; in this example, changing the thermostat causes the furnace to activate.

D is incorrect because when systems are interconnected, a change in one system causes a change in the other system; in this example, the blender does not cause another technological system to change.

12. B

A is incorrect because before they can use their modeling skills, the designers have to research the answer to a question.

B is correct because answering this question will require the design team to research similar models that had been created in the past.

C is incorrect because before they can use their mathematics skills to create the model, the designers have to research the answer to a question.

D is incorrect because brainstorming skills are unlikely to provide definitive answers to a factual question such as the one the design team needs answered.

13. D

A is incorrect because a meterstick is intended to measure much smaller distances than the length of a bridge.

B is incorrect because a meterstick is intended to measure dimensions, not weight.

C is incorrect because a meterstick is intended to measure dimensions, not speed.

D is correct because a meterstick is intended to measure relatively small dimensions, such as the length, width, and height of a shelf.

14. A

A is correct because the beginning temperature is the input that goes into the system and results in an output, or a different temperature.

B is incorrect because the thermostat is the control; it regulates the heating and cooling system of the home.

C is incorrect because an output is something that comes out of a system. The resulting temperature of the home is the output.

D is incorrect because a feedback is something that happens within a system and that may cause the system to adjust.

15. A

A is correct because the organism (algae) is creating something (oil) that people incorporate into their technology (biofuel).

B is incorrect because people use milk produced by cow's for nutritional purposes, not technological purposes.

C is incorrect because the bird inspires engineers to give the train a certain shape, but the bird is not actually part of the technological process.

D is incorrect because technology is threatening the bear, but the bear is not contributing to the technological process.

Critical Thinking

16.

- identify material and improved technology (e.g., *Steel was a modified material made from iron and carbon*; etc.)

- argument for whether this material added value to society (e.g., *The invention of steel caused the Steel Age, an age when steel was used in just about every technological application. It added value because it improved building infrastructure and increased economic development*; etc.)

Extended Response

17.

- correctly filled-in Pugh chart:

	Ease of Use	Size	Speed	Total
Techn-ology A	2	0	1	3
Techn-ology B	1	1	0	2
Techn-ology C	0	0	1	1
Techn-ology D	1	1	2	4

- technology D plus explanation (e.g., *Its values add up to 4, the highest of all the options; Technology D most closely resembles the criteria*; etc.)

- identify additional factors to include in chart (e.g., *cost; availability; degree of hazard*; etc.)

Unit Test B

Key Concepts

1. A	6. B	11. C
2. B	7. A	12. D
3. C	8. A	13. C
4. D	9. C	14. B
5. B	10. B	15. D

1. A

A is correct because material A transfers electric current well.

B is incorrect because material B is brittle and does not transfer electric current well.

C is incorrect because material C has a low melting point and does not transfer electric current well.

D is incorrect because some exotic materials may work, but the properties of the example here includes low conductivity.

2. B

A is incorrect because a desert is part of the natural world, not the designed world.

B is correct because a city is part of the designed world.

C is incorrect because a mountain is part of the natural world, not the designed world.

D is incorrect because a rainforest is part of the natural world, not the designed world.

3. C

A is incorrect because cell phones that feature different colors, shapes, and ring tones are examples of technology changing to create new wants.

B is incorrect because smaller computers that can perform more operations are examples of technology changing to become more efficient.

C is correct because solar cells are examples of technology changing in response to the problem of polluting, nonrenewable energy resources.

D is incorrect because video editing software is an example of new technology being developed to support or better utilize already existing technology.

4. D

A is incorrect because the bullet train does not help the kingfisher with its life processes.

B is incorrect because the kingfisher is not being used in a technological process (e.g., cleaning up oil, treating wastewater, etc.).

C is incorrect because a bird (kingfisher) would not likely be genetically modified to resemble the characteristics of a train.

D is correct because the structure of the kingfisher's beak is an example of an organism's structure being used to develop new technology (the bullet train).

5. B

A is incorrect because a trade-off is the giving up of one thing in return for another.

B is correct because factors that limit the design of a product are called constraints.

C is incorrect because a prototype is a test model of a product.

D is incorrect because methodical thinking is a skill used in the design process.

6. B

A is incorrect because the ability to communicate over long distances by telephone has a direct effect on society more than it has on the environment.

B is correct because air pollution caused by

technology has a negative effect on the environment.

C is incorrect because the invention of the steam and internal combustion engine is a better example of how new technology often drives the development of newer technology.

D is incorrect because vicariously exploring far-off environments through technology does not have a direct effect on those environments.

7. A

A is correct because adaptive technologies are used to help organisms complete life processes, such as those ordinarily performed by a person's kidneys.

B is incorrect because adaptive technologies are used to help organisms complete life processes; storing digital music and documents is not a life process.

C is incorrect because adaptive technologies are used to help organisms complete life processes; transporting heavy materials is not a life process.

D is incorrect because adaptive technologies are used to help organisms complete life processes; studying microscopic organisms is not a life process.

8. A

A is correct because a car has the highest total, making it the best option to choose

B is incorrect because a train has a value of 7, 2 points lower than the best option.

C is incorrect because an airplane has a value of 6, 3 points lower than the best option.

D is incorrect because walking has a value of 3, 6 points lower than the best option.

9. C

A is incorrect because this is a trade-off in which the negative effect of the drug (the flu-like symptoms) is outweighed by the positive effect (keeping the disease at bay).

B is incorrect because this is a trade-off in which the negative effect of the drug (the flu-like symptoms) is outweighed by the positive effect (keeping the disease at bay).

C is correct because this is a trade-off in which the negative effect of the drug (the flu-like symptoms) is outweighed by the positive effect (keeping the disease at bay).

D is incorrect because this is a trade-off in which the negative effect of the drug (the flu-like symptoms) is outweighed by the positive effect (keeping the disease at bay).

10. B

A is incorrect because a mouse inputs data into a computer.

B is correct because a printer outputs data from a computer.

C is incorrect because electricity is an input to make the computer run.

D is incorrect because a keyboard is another device that inputs data to a computer.

11. C

A is incorrect because when systems are interconnected, a change in one system causes a change in the other system; in this example, no technological systems cause other systems to change.

B is incorrect because when systems are interconnected, a change in one system causes a change in the other system; in this example, the bicycle does not cause another technological system to change.

C is correct because when systems are interconnected, a change in one system causes a change in the other system; in this example, executing a function on the computer causes the printer to activate.

D is incorrect because when systems are interconnected, a change in one system causes a change in the other system; in this example, the oven does not cause another technological system to change.

12. D

A is incorrect because mathematical skills are needed more than research skills to calculate speed.

B is incorrect because computer skills are needed more than research skills to create a computer model.

C is incorrect because brainstorming skills are needed more than research skills to imagine new ideas.

D is correct because research skills are typically necessary to learn factual information about the past.

13. C

A is incorrect because future effects of a weather system cannot physically be observed; a cyber tool such as a computer program is more appropriate for this use.

B is incorrect because complex natural phenomena that happened thousands of years ago cannot physically be observed; a cyber tool such as a computer program is more appropriate for this use.

C is correct because skeletons are physical objects that can easily be studied and represented using physical tools.

D is incorrect because volcanic eruptions are dangerous events; a cyber tool such as a computer program would be a safer way to model volcanic eruptions.

14. B

A is incorrect because an input is something that goes into the system. The thermostat is not the input of these systems.

B is correct because the thermostat is the control; it regulates the heating and cooling system of the home.

C is incorrect because an output is something that comes out of a system. The thermostat is not the output of these systems.

D is incorrect because feedback is a type of input received by a control system.

15. D

A is incorrect because the yeast is not changed by baking technology.

B is incorrect because the yeast is not being used to create technology.

C is incorrect because the yeast is not being used to help another organism achieve its life processes.

D is correct because the organism produce gas bubbles, which make the bread dough rise. Upon baking, the yeast dies, but the pockets of bubbles are left, creating a soft and spongy texture that is characteristic of bread.

Critical Thinking
16.

- one way to incorporate modified materials into a bridge design (e.g., *The design team might try to modify different metals to see whether they can develop a stronger metal, a more durable metal, a less expensive metal*; etc.)

- explanation of how this use of modified materials would be beneficial (e.g., *Modifying materials to make them stronger or more durable would allow the team to build a longer-lasting bridge that can hold more weight; Modifying materials to make them less expensive would allow the team to build the bridge for less money*; etc.)

Extended Response
17.

- correctly filled-in Pugh chart:

	Ease of Use	Size	Speed	Total
Techno-logy A	1	1	2	4
Techno-logy B	1	0	1	2
Techno-logy C	1	0	0	1
Techno-logy D	2	0	1	3

- technology C plus explanation (e.g., *Its values add up to 1, the lowest of all the options; Technology C least closely meets the criteria*; etc.)

- identify additional factor that could not be analyzed by a Pugh Chart (e.g., *The technology recommended by the Pugh chart might not be available where I live, or it might be too expensive for me to afford. In that case, I would have to ignore the recommendations of the Pugh chart for more practical concerns*; etc.)

End-of-Module Test

1. A	11. B	21. A
2. B	12. C	22. D
3. A	13. A	23. B
4. C	14. B	24. C
5. A	15. A	25. B
6. D	16. A	26. C
7. D	17. D	27. B
8. A	18. B	28. B
9. D	19. A	29. D
10. C	20. C	30. B

1. A See Unit 1, Lesson 2

A is correct because having other scientists perform the experiment will determine if it can be replicated and happen with frequency.

B is incorrect because if the scientists change the procedure, they cannot be sure if the conditions of the first procedure are replicated by the second procedure.

C is incorrect because it does not check the validity of the experiment.

D is incorrect because this step tests how the medicines react to the bacteria but does not test the validity of the original experiment.

2. B See Unit 1, Lesson 3

A is incorrect because the three drawings clearly show that atomic models have varied over time.

B is correct because as scientists learned more about atoms through experimentation and observation, they modified the atomic model to match their discoveries.

C is incorrect because the dates on the models indicate that they show a progression of the atomic models.

D is incorrect because the dates on the models indicate that they show a progression of the atomic models.

3. A See Unit 1, Lesson 4

A is correct because Forde works with students in their

classrooms to stimulate their interest in math and science.

B   is incorrect because Forde works as a role model in schools, not as an astronomer.

C   is incorrect because the passage mentions only mathematics, oceanography, and earth science.

D   is incorrect because no information is provided to suggest that Forde is involved in conserving energy resources or developing new ones.

4.   C See Unit 2, Lesson 3

A   is incorrect because a train would best be represented by a physical model.

B   is incorrect because a building would best be represented by a scale model.

C   is correct because the water cycle would best be represented by a conceptual model such as a diagram.

D   is incorrect because a formula would best be represented by a mathematical model.

5.   A See Unit 3, Lesson 2

A   is correct because a life-cycle analysis often focuses on the effects of technology on the environment.

B   is incorrect because there is no indication that something has been lost for the gain of the environment.

C   is incorrect because there is no indication that the company's design was influenced by an analysis of risks and benefits.

D   is incorrect because this is a very general term that does not apply to a couch.

6.   D See Unit 2, Lesson 3

A   is incorrect because none of the models implies bigger or smaller atoms.

B   is incorrect because the current model of the atom shows several different kinds of particles in the atom's center.

C   is incorrect because no model shows positively charged particles moving about a negatively charged center.

D   is correct because as scientists learned more about atoms, they discovered that atoms had positively charged centers that were surrounded by clouds of electrons.

7.   D See Unit 1, Lesson 4

A   is incorrect because people in all professions and fields work hard.

B   is incorrect because people in all professions and fields solve problems as part of their work.

C   is incorrect because nothing in the illustration suggests that the person is thinking about the next step.

D   is correct because scientists use tools to help them make observations.

8.   A See Unit 1, Lesson 1

A   is correct because scientists use creativity to design experiments.

B   is incorrect because skepticism is not the principal trait used by scientists in

designing an experiment. Scientists typically use skepticism after designing the experiment—for example, when making repeated observations, replicating experiments, and examining experimental designs and conclusions.

C   is incorrect because objectivity is not the principal trait used by scientists in designing an experiment. Scientists depend upon objectivity when recording information so as not to allow personal bias to influence the process.

D   is incorrect because determination is not the principal trait used by scientists in designing an experiment. Scientists may be determined to complete an investigation so that the question may be answered or the problem solved.

9.   D See Unit 2, Lesson 3

A   is incorrect because a chemical formula uses numbers, letters, and mathematical symbols to represent a chemical reaction.

B   is incorrect because a chemical formula uses numbers, letters, and mathematical symbols to represent a chemical reaction.

C   is incorrect because a chemical formula uses numbers, letters, and mathematical symbols to represent a chemical reaction.

D is correct because a chemical formula uses numbers, letters, and mathematical symbols to represent a chemical reaction.

10. C See Unit 3, Lesson 4

A is incorrect because these items are made out of plastic, a type of polymer.

B is incorrect because these items are made out of plastic, a type of polymer.

C is correct because these items are made out of plastic, a type of polymer.

D is incorrect because these items are made out of plastic, a type of polymer.

11. B See Unit 3, Lesson 4

A is incorrect because this example does not describe how titanium has been tested; it describe how it has been used.

B is correct because this example describes how titanium can be modified to maximize its desirable properties.

C is incorrect because this example does not describe a material that is limited by the cost of extracting it.

D is incorrect because this example does not describe titanium's properties (other than that it is a strong material).

12. C See Unit 3, Lesson 3

A is incorrect because a car is an open system with inputs and outputs.

B is incorrect because an oven is an open system with inputs and outputs.

C is correct because a snowglobe is a self-contained system that is closed off from most inputs and outputs.

D is incorrect because a food processor is an open system with inputs and outputs.

13. A See Unit 2, Lesson 1

A is correct because in 2007, the population was 6,000, and in 2008, the population was 5,500. This is a decrease of 500 people.

B is incorrect because in 2007, the population was 6,000, and in 2008, the population was 5,500. This is a decrease of 500 people, not 1,000 people.

C is incorrect because in 2007, the population was 6,000, and in 2008, the population was 5,500. This is a decrease of 500 people, not 1,500 people.

D is incorrect because in 2007, the population was 6,000, and in 2008, the population was 5,500. This is a decrease of 500 people, not 2,000 people.

14. B See Unit 1, Lesson 1

A is incorrect because although pseudoscience resembles science, it does not follow scientific methods.

B is correct because pseudoscience does not follow scientific methods.

C is incorrect because pseudoscience resembles science, but does not follow scientific methods.

D is incorrect because pseudoscience resembles science.

15. A See Unit 2, Lesson 1

A is correct because the figure is a visual representation of an atom and therefore is a model.

B is incorrect because a hypothesis is an attempt to explain observed phenomena.

C is incorrect because an experiment consists of various steps designed to answer a question.

D is incorrect because an observation is something a scientist takes note of to collect information.

16. A See Unit 2, Lesson 2

A is correct because eight zeroes should follow the number 3.

B is incorrect because eight zeroes should follow the number 3.

C is incorrect because eight zeroes should follow the number 3.

D is incorrect because eight zeroes should follow the number 3.

17. D See Unit 1, Lesson 1

A is incorrect because a hypothesis offers a possible explanation, but a hypothesis is used to identify test variables and issues to be explored. The hypothesis itself does not support an explanation.

B is incorrect because scientists must never allow personal bias or opinions to affect the nature of their work.

C is incorrect because imagination and originality because a hypothesis is used to identify test variables and issues to be explored. The hypothesis itself does not support an explanation.

D is correct because the data obtained from objective measurements can be used to reach a valid conclusion.

18. B See Unit 2, Lesson 1

A is incorrect because the table provides no temperature data.

B is correct because there are more hours of daylight, as shown in the table.

C is incorrect because from January to July, the sun rises earlier, not later, in the morning.

D is incorrect because from January to July, the sun sets later, not earlier, in the evening.

19. A See Unit 2, Lesson 2

A is correct because a simulation is a program that can analyze data to make predictions based on trends of an event.

B is incorrect because the biologist graphing data from direct observations represents the current situation, but does not clearly predict events that have not happened yet.

C is incorrect because the biologist cannot observe in real-time events that have not happened yet.

D is incorrect because the biologist cannot use indirect observations to make a reasonable prediction about events that have not happened yet.

20. C See Unit 3, Lesson 5

A is incorrect because adaptive technologies are used to help organisms complete life processes; by helping to restore people's health, medicines also help organisms complete life processes.

B is incorrect because adaptive technologies are used to help organisms complete life processes; by helping to restore people's health, medicines also help organisms complete life processes.

C is correct because adaptive technologies are used to help organisms complete life processes; by helping to restore people's health, medicines also help organisms complete life processes.

D is incorrect because adaptive technologies are used to help organisms complete life processes; by helping to restore people's health, medicines also help organisms complete life processes.

21. A See Unit 1, Lesson 2

A is correct because the data shows that when exposed to equal amounts of solar energy, the metal pieces absorb different amounts of heat. Color is the independent variable. The varying amounts of absorbed heat energy produce different temperatures.

B is incorrect because all the metal pieces are placed in direct sunlight.

C is incorrect because the masses of the metal pieces are identical.

D is incorrect because the metal pieces are identical at the beginning of the experiment.

22. D See Unit 3, Lesson 6

A is incorrect because the company is investing more money in "going green," so it is not likely concerned about money.

B is incorrect because there is no indication that cultural practices affected this decision.

C is incorrect because there is no indication that societal norms affected this decision.

D is correct because "green" actions are typically motivated by concern for protecting the environment.

23. B See Unit 1, Lesson 1

A is incorrect because the new information may support the existing theory.

B is correct because scientists must reevaluate the theory to determine whether it needs to be revised as a result of the new information.

C is incorrect because the new information may cause the existing theory to be discarded.

D is incorrect because the new information may cause scientists to modify or even discard the existing theory.

24. C See Unit 2, Lesson 2

A is incorrect because the measurements are close together (precise), but they are not close to the actual value (not accurate).

B is incorrect because the measurements are close together (precise), but they are not close to the actual value (not accurate).

C is correct because the measurements are close together (precise), but they are not close to the actual value (not accurate).

D is incorrect because the measurements are close together (precise), but they are not close to the actual value (not accurate).

25. B See Unit 3, Lesson 1

A is incorrect because engineering is the application of science and mathematics to solve real-life problems.

B is correct because engineering is the application of science and mathematics to solve real-life problems.

C is incorrect because technology is the application of science for practical purposes.

D is incorrect because technologies are the result of engineering and science.

26. C See Unit 3, Lesson 3

A is incorrect because a control is a mechanism for regulating a system, not an interaction.

B is incorrect because a component is a part of a system, not an interaction.

C is correct because the loudspeaker will continue to produce louder and louder sound, an example of a positive feedback.

D is incorrect because the loudspeaker would produce an increasingly quieter sound if the interaction were an example of negative feedback.

27. B See Unit 3, Lesson 1

A is incorrect because defining the problems requires the scientist to sit down and write out the problem.

B is correct because the library contains many resources that can help a scientist conduct scientific research.

C is incorrect because testing and evaluating would most likely be done in the lab.

D is incorrect because communicating the results would most likely be done with the help of a computer or some other device.

28. B See Unit 3, Lesson 5

A is incorrect because the plants are being changed to resist disease, not to participate in a technological process.

B is correct because plants have been changed to become more resistant to disease.

C is incorrect because selective breeding is not creating new technologies inspired by natural structures.

D is incorrect because these plants have not been developed into a new technology.

29. D See Unit 3, Lesson 2

A is incorrect because the actual sales of this product were neither expected nor favorable; they were well below the expected number in every year.

B is incorrect because the actual sales were unfavorable, but they were also unexpected, as they were well below the expected number in every year.

C is incorrect because the actual sales were unexpected, but they were also unfavorable as the product did not make nearly as much money as was projected.

D is correct because the sales are both unexpected and unfavorable, because the actual sales line is well below the expected sales line for every year.

30. B See Unit 3, Lesson 4

A is incorrect because susceptibility to corrosion is a type of chemical property.

B is correct because susceptibility to corrosion is a type of chemical property.

C   is incorrect because
     susceptibility to corrosion is a
     type of chemical property.

D   is incorrect because
     susceptibility to corrosion is a
     type of chemical property.